Soul Seeing

Light ✧ Love ✧ Forgiveness

Soul Seeing

Light ✧ Love ✧ Forgiveness

Michael Leach and Friends

ORBIS BOOKS
Maryknoll, New York 10545

Manufactured in the United States of America.
Manuscript editing and typesetting by Joan Weber Laflamme.

Library of Congress Cataloging-in-Publication Data

Names: Leach, Michael, editor.
Title: Soul seeing : light-love-forgiveness / [edited by] Michael Leach and Friends.
Description: Maryknoll, New York : Orbis Books, [2018] | Includes bibliographical references and index.
Identifiers: LCCN 2018014165 | ISBN 9781626982956 (pbk)
Subjects: LCSH: Christian life—Catholic authors—Anecdotes. | Spiritual life—Catholic Church—Anecdotes.
Classification: LCC BX2350.3 .S643 2018 | DDC 242—dc23 LC record available at https://lccn.loc.gov/2018014165

For Gramma Lou, who first taught me to see,
for Fr. Burrill and Larry McCauley,
who taught me what to see,
and for Dr. Hora, who made it clearer the rest of the way.
Thank you.

We see God through the same eye God sees us. Our eye and God's are one—one seeing, one knowing, one love.

—MEISTER ECKHART

Contents

Part One
Light

Part Two
Love

✧ Sɪɢʜᴛɪɴɢ ✧
The Little Prince Tells You a Secret
Antoine de Saint-Exupéry

**Part Three
Forgiveness**

38

The Day I Stood Shimmering in Shame
Brian Doyle

39

The Gift of Being Brought to Our Knees
and Forgiven for Our Sins
Heather King

40

Sin Makes Guilt and Guilt Makes Fear,
and Fear and Guilt Make More Sin
Michael Leach

✧ Sɪɢʜᴛɪɴɢ ✧
How the Light Gets In
Leonard Cohen

Preface

It is seven years since *Soul Seeing* first appeared with the column "Christ and Cerebral Palsy." I quoted Dr. Thomas Hora, a psychiatrist who was the best spiritual teacher I ever had:

> There is more to us than meets the eye. We all have the faculty to discern spiritual qualities in the world. We can see beauty; we can see integrity; we can see honesty; we can see love; we can see goodness; we can see joy; we can see peace; we can see harmony; we can see intelligence; and so forth. None of these things has any form; none of these things can be imagined; none of these things is tangible, and yet they can be seen. What is the organ that sees these invisible things? Some people call it the soul, spirit, or consciousness. Man is a spiritual being endowed with spiritual faculties of perception.

I ended the column with a prayer:

> Jesus, the next time I see someone with what doctors call cerebral palsy or Down syndrome, give me the

eyes to see what is really there: wholeness, innocence, perfect health, love, joy, intelligence, and abundant beauty. Help me know, right now: when I look at anyone, I am looking at myself, I am looking at *you*, because all of us, each of us, are spiritual aspects of you and only you. God bless everyone! I close my eyes now and remember someone I've passed by or ignored and ask you to see love for me. I am learning that I can behold you and everyone with the same eyes that you see us. I am going to sit still now, listen—and *see*.

Soul Seeing began with a phone call from the editors of the *National Catholic Reporter.* They asked if I'd be interested in writing a regular column. I brought up soul seeing as a way of looking at life in a way not much explored in the pages of NCR or anywhere. I suggested that I write one column every month or two and, for diversity, ask friends to write the others. They asked for a brief description. I sent this:

This biweekly column is about seeing God, the world, and ourselves with the eye of the soul. It is not about changing the world but changing the way we see the world. Each column is a spiritual reflection on the beauty that hides behind appearances and the peace that is beyond all understanding.

Since then more than 160 *Soul Seeing* columns have invited readers to perceive the spiritual that is within us and around us: to see the kingdom of heaven in a car wash, hear the music of life on an R train, taste Eucharist in a basket of biscuits shared by famished children in Ethiopia, and feel the touch of angels' wings in the stillness of a radiation room. We have endeavored to read the Bible with the eye of the soul and listen to the "still, small voice of God" with the same ear God hears us. We stretched our souls with the "old yoga ladies" at a senior center in Hastings on Hudson and danced with a leper in Africa as she danced in gratitude for a new bed. We embraced hugs as an outward sign of inner grace and, God help us, even sipped Scotch at midnight with Morrie, the lovable bishop of Paris, Kansas. Each column has encouraged us to do just one thing: cultivate this sixth sense God has implanted in each of us, a GPS system back to Eden we call "soul seeing."

This book selects 56 columns from among the 160. Their purpose is to open our eyes to the light that bathes life with grace, feel the love of God that beats in our hearts and never stops, and touch each other with the forgiveness that makes all things new. It is about seeing the world as a sacrament and being in the world as an instrument of grace.

Soul seeing is as old and comfortable as the tunic Paul wore on his visits to the Christian communities. "Don't be interested in the troubles you can see now," he told them, "but be interested in the things that cannot be seen. For the things you see now will soon be gone, but the things you cannot see will last forever." What lasts forever is spiritual: truth, love, mercy, goodness, beauty, harmony, humility, compassion, gratitude, joy, peace, salvation.

St. Augustine in the fourth century knew what Paul was talking about. "Late have I loved thee, O Beauty so ancient and so new," he cried, "late have I loved you! You flashed, you shone, and you dispelled my blindness!" It is never too late to experience the grace of soul seeing.

In the thirteenth century St. Bonaventure encouraged students to see with the soul. In the nineteenth the poet Gerard Manley Hopkins showed us "the dearest freshness deep down things," and in the twentieth Teilhard de Chardin asked us to look through appearances and contemplate "the chosen part of things." Dr. Hora defined prayer as "an endeavor to behold what is real" and inspired his students to pray the prayer of beholding. Despite appearances, he taught, and even in suffering, we have the capacity to behold "peace, assurance, gratitude, and love."

We may not be able to go out and change the world. But we can be still and change the way we see the world. That is what makes all the difference. And changes everything.

Acknowledgments

The *National Catholic Reporter*, where these columns appeared, is an independent, lay run, religious news source for Catholics and others who are interested in the crossroad where moral, social, and spiritual values intersect. Since 1964 it has been a voice for the voiceless and the marginalized, and has told prophetic stories that others dared not. *Soul Seeing*, begun in 2011, was another step forward in expressing the spiritual values that hold all of us, religious or not, together as one.

I am grateful to NCR's renowned publisher and editor Tom Fox for asking me to write a column and for giving me the go ahead to begin something new. I am equally grateful to his current successor as publisher Caitlin Hedlin and editor Dennis Coday, who were part of the original conversations and have encouraged me ever since. The old building in Kansas City where NCR workers do their mission has always been a seed bed for talent and dedication. I'd like to thank my other biweekly partners: managing editor Stephanie Yeagle; special sections editor/photo coordinator/copy chief Teresa Malcolm; layout editor/art director Toni-Ann Ortiz; web editor Mick Forgey; artist

Pat Marin; and everyone else on the NCR masthead. Tom Roberts, former editor now retired, like Tom Fox has been a friend for the longest time.

I am grateful to all the guest columnists to *Soul Seeing*. My initial plan was to call on author/friends I had published over a five-decade career in book publishing, but before you knew it new writers were submitting essays and, as it says in Genesis, they were very good. I was also able to pursue a lifelong interest in seeking out new young writers and several have made their debut on the pages of NCR

All of the *Soul Seeing* columns are on the NCR website at https://www.ncronline.org/columns/soul-seeing and appeared in the *National Catholic Reporter* in the *Soul Seeing* column, recipient of the first-place award for "best regular column on spirituality" by the Catholic Press Association for the past four years. The date of publication follows each essay herein.

Thanks to Robert Ellsberg, publisher of Orbis Books, for asking me to do this book, to Roberta Savage for her beautiful cover design, to Joan Laflamme for her first-class, reader-friendly book design, and to Maria Angelini for shepherding the manuscript with her usual love to the living creature you hold in your hands.

Soul Seeing

Light ✧ Love ✧ Forgiveness

PART ONE

LIGHT

Awake, sleeper, rise from the dead, and
Christ will give you light.

—EPHESIANS 5:14

I Was Blind and Then I Saw

Alice Camille

I saw him from a block away. He perched precariously in a motorized chair, his body slight like a child's, hardly weighing fifty pounds in his maturity. I counted three serpentine bends in the arm that reached out to guide his odyssey, and my heart sank at the writhing distress that was this man's whole existence. His limbs twisted like a contortionist. Even his face was beyond his control, gripped by grimaces many times a minute.

I wondered what it would be like, not to be able to smile.

Religion primes us to contemplate exalted ideas like incarnation. In the books incarnation makes the things of eternity present and tangible. But on the street incarnation is rarely so kind. It seldom includes divine infants pitched softly into a bed of straw or heavenly hosts crooning sweet Glorias. There may have been one holy night when stars were brightly shining; there are uncounted un-holy ones, where the darkness is doubly dark. Incarnation, as we learn to live with it, too often looks more like this: solitary suffering on a street devoid of angel song.

Perhaps this is why, much of the time, making eternity tangible is the least of our concerns. We may even prefer the reverse phenomenon: to make the tactile world considerably less concrete. It's hard to see past the walls of our isolating realities. And when that reality is painful, life is a prison. The physical routinely prejudices, intimidates, or defeats us before we say hello. Yet we follow a guide who saw past "tax collector" and "prostitute" to the man and woman struggling behind these masks. Even male and female isn't supposed to matter anymore—or insider, outsider, free or in chains. Liberation begins in the eyes, if those old stories mean anything. Genuine sight is something we can't do without. Yet it's also something we're blind to—until someone, with great affection, smears mud into our eyes.

Standing there on the street that day, I was resolved *not* to see. The thought of meeting this man was an affliction. Such complete suffering was intolerable to witness. I didn't want to risk even the casual encounter of passing him on the sidewalk. I decided to cross to the other side of the street, which would have been simple enough to do. It would have seemed innocent. More than that, it would preserve my innocence from contact with a stranger's misery. I wouldn't risk meeting his eyes or sharing even for an instant his reality. I did not want to know more about such anguish than was visible from a distance.

Moral cowardice isn't something we like to admit about ourselves. So as the impulse to avoid this man engulfed me,

I wrestled with it. He wasn't asking for anything. All we owe to each other in this world is the recognition of our common humanity. Passing a man on the street would take but a moment. Could I not give a fellow human being one instant of respect?

Heart trembling, I walked forward. And as this stranger and I entered that delicate zone of closeness where people acknowledge each other, I looked into his eyes and managed a small greeting, a timid smile. It was then that the kingdom of God broke through. This stranger, with his labored movements, attempted a smile out of one corner of his mouth. A crooked little half grin zigzagged across his face like a dancing sun peeping out from behind a cloud. The warmth, joy, and delight spreading across his features transfigured him before my eyes. Or perhaps: I changed. Suddenly I recognized his humor, his twinkling eyes, and his excruciating beauty as a fellow traveler in the world. Light poured out from him and over me and into the street until it covered the whole scene like a radiant blanket. It took no more than an instant, a quick smile and a greeting, but as he passed by and the sound of his motorized chair buzzed further down the street, I broke into tears. I nearly knelt on the sidewalk. *O my God, it was Jesus*—and I almost missed him.

DECEMBER 23, 2011

2

Know What Your Duty Is, Do It without Hesitation

Michael Leach

Last night Vickie and I watched a documentary about Leonard Cohen on Netflix. Cohen was a Canadian musician who became a Buddhist monk and wrote unforgettable songs like *Halleluja*. In the documentary he tells a story from the Bhagavad Gita about a general named Arjuna who did not want to kill others in a righteous war against evil. "The general," says Cohen in his deep and soothing voice, "that great general. He's standing in his chariot. And all the chariots are readied for war. And across the valley he sees his opponents. And there he sees not just uncles and aunts and cousins, he sees gurus, he sees teachers that have taught him. He sees them. And Krishna, an expression of the deity, says to him, 'You will never untangle the circumstances that brought you to this moment. You are a warrior. Embrace your destiny, your fate. Know what your duty is. Do it with love in your heart. And do it without hesitation.'"

The Gita is a myth that teaches truths about ourselves, the roles we regret and try to forget, the faces we try on that crack and crumble like Halloween masks, and the indestructible Self we really are that never dies because it is never born and always lives. Cohen, channeling Krishna, says to Arjuna, "Understand that they (personas) have already been killed, and so have you. This is just a play. This is my will. You're caught up in the circumstances that I determine for you. So arise! Stand up and do your duty."

As the documentary continues, Bono and Beth Orton and Rufus Wainwright and others sing Cohen songs that once you hear you never forget: *Tower of Song . . . Anthem* ("There is a crack, a crack in everything. That's how the light gets in") . . . *I'm Your Man*.

"I'm your man." I could never remember all the circumstances that brought me to the place fifteen years ago where Vickie began to remember nothing, including how to eat with a spoon. But I do remember a moment fifty years ago lying in bed in a rectory in the middle of the night, lonely and not wanting to be a priest anymore. I didn't have what it takes to go the course. I thought how comforting it would be to go to bed each night and wake up each morning with a woman at my side whom I loved and who loved me and how my singular duty would be to love and protect her till death do us part, even if she got sick before I did and I'd have to take care of her for the rest of my life. I asked God for a miracle and said if I broke my vow to be a priest forever I would never break this one. I would be her man, in sickness and in health.

Did I know then that Vickie, an embodiment of intelligence, would get Alzheimer's at fifty-seven? Was the message to me, be careful of what you wish for because you might get it? Or was it, embrace your destiny? Know what your duty is. And do it without hesitation. For a while I shook my fist at God like Job. Fifteen years later I have come to know: my calling is to be here with Vickie as she forgets the lines in the play and becomes more and more the divine expression she really is.

I'm good with it. The last few years have been among the best of my life.

In the morning our caregiver Silvia is here to help Vickie bathe and get dressed and to feed her breakfast. We're at the kitchen table, me in front of the sliding glass door to the patio. Just behind it is a garden Vickie tended for thirty years. Half buried in snow is a statue of Sister Mary Southard's Our Lady of the Garden. Vickie sits next to me by the big center window with a direct view to a Buddha statue that sits under a cherry tree with Christmas ornaments tinkling in the wind on its naked branches. Silvia brings a bowl of Life cereal (with cinnamon) topped by strawberries to Vickie, then sits at her side and feeds her loving spoonsful. Vickie gazes at Silvia as a baby regards her mother, never looking away, eyes full of trust.

"Vickie *linda*," says Silvia, who is from Venezuela. "*Eres mi Buda.*"

"She's your Buddha?" I ask her.

"She teaches me. She's my Master. She shows me that life is from inside. Some people they have all things money can buy but no peace. They look at Vickie, they think maybe she is broken, but you look inside and you see light and her light shines everywhere. Vickie *linda*, she has beautiful life."

"That's beautiful, Silvia. I'm used to thinking I'm here for her, but she's here for me too. We're teaching each other, aren't we?" I talk to Vickie, "We have a good life, huh, Sweetheart?"

Vickie nods. "Thank oo," she says. She understands everything until her brain starts to get tired around 10 o'clock. You can't tell by her tired appearance late in the day, but the eye of your soul still sees all the intelligence in the universe glowing inside her.

"Silvia, what you say about Vickie being your Master makes me remember: did I ever tell you what a psychiatrist taught me about the statue of the Buddha and the statue of the Thinker?"

"Thinker?"

"It's a statue by Rodin of a tortured soul. A naked man bent in an uncomfortable position, with his right elbow on his left thigh and his hand holding up his chin. Every muscle in his body is tense. His face is a fist. He's thinking, calculating, trying to figure everything out. Then there is the statue of the Buddha."

We look outside the window at Mister Buddha, as we all call him, who presides over a concrete bowl of icy water pecked at by a bluebird. A couple of squirrels join in.

"See how the Buddha just sits there, eyes closed, not thinking about anything but contemplating everything. His hands on his lap, every muscle relaxed. But he has large ears and hears our suffering. He sees us and gives us all his calm, his peace, and his peace increases and he gives us more, like a fountain that keeps spilling over. That's why I put him there, where Vickie can see what he represents from her favorite chair. I want her to see peace."

"*Vickie es la señora Buda*," says Silvia.

"She is. And I'm Mr. Thinker." We laugh.

We're quiet now. I think again of Our Lady of the Garden, the mother of God who also sits in peace, on a rock in the snow, just waiting for the flowers to rise again. I appreciate that the flowers that come to us in spring were already killed and the flowers absent in winter never died. "Look at the flowers," Jesus said. "Just look. They don't fuss or worry or obsess. But I tell you, not even Solomon in all his glory was adorned like one of these." That brings to mind the song *Don't Worry. Be Happy,* and then something Dr. Thomas Hora, the psychiatrist, used to say, "Everything everywhere is already alright." Thoughts bounce around my head like balls in a pinball machine. I remember a quote from Meister Eckhart: "We are all meant to be mothers of God."

Silvia is washing the dishes. Vickie is looking at me. Her look creates a little crack in my brain. Don't think about it. Just do your duty.

I take the green bib from Vickie's neck and wipe a strawberry stain from her lips. "I love you," I say. "I love *oo*," she says.

3

Seeing the Music of Life

Michael Morwood

On Christmas Eve, Maria and I attended the American Ballet Theatre's presentation of *The Nutcracker* in New York. Ballet is not high on my list of entertainments, but on this occasion I was profoundly moved. What inspired me was not just the work of art, but the way I found myself present to it, taking it in, living in it. I wondered at whatever is at work in the universe, hurtling atoms billions of years ago into the life and death of countless stars, through transformation after transformation into Tchaikovsky, such astonishing music, into the beauty and grace of the dancers, and in me reflecting on how this all happens.

On New Year's Day I went for a long walk on the Appalachian Trail (honest) and listened for a time to *The World's Greatest Operatic Arias*. The music led me to reflect on Verdi, Mozart, and others and the question: Where does this music come from? And how can Joan Sutherland, Pavarotti, and other singers give such wonderful expression to the music? What is going on here? I concluded that Tchaikovsky and Mozart did not add anything to the universe through their music. Rather, the universe found a way through them to give expression to itself.

I was moved again by a sense of wonder, and was grateful to be human, to be a conscious aspect of God's astonishing universe.

Jesus so appreciated the kingdom of heaven right before him and manifested gratitude in the very way he looked at the lilies of the field, the birds of the air, people. I see him inviting me to manifest wonder and appreciation in my own life. Here and now in the twenty-first century I can marvel at the way atoms and stardust are transformed into the life form we are. I imagine Jesus saying to me, "Michael, the human enterprise and the universe in which it has come to be is God-charged. You not only give the universe a way of manifesting itself, you give God, the Ground of all Being, a way of coming to expression. That is what it means to be human: to express light, love, beauty, harmony, goodness, peace. Take in this good news about yourself and everyone else, and *see*. See everything around you with the eye of your soul. See the music of life!"

I have sought for years to learn more and more about the contemporary scientific data about our universe and our human origins—and it motivates me to see the world around me as Jesus wants me to see it. I see what I have always been led to see and believe—that Jesus embodied the Divine Presence in human form. When I bring his story to the scientific story about our human origins and how life evolved on earth I'm led to a new awareness and appreciation of the Divine Presence all around me, a love that bonds all that exists. I think it was this awareness and appreciation that drove Jesus when he preached about "the kingdom of God." He wanted people to see what he saw: people giving human expression to the Divine in their living and loving.

I also see Jesus differently now. I see him as revealer of God-always-here-with-us, rather than as a gateway to a God in the heavens. I see myself differently. I am not living in exile from God. Far from it. I have this wonderful opportunity—my lifetime—to give human expression to the universe and to the Divine Presence charging it. I see the world around me differently. I see the task of the church differently. I see prayer and sacraments differently. Instead of looking for an Elsewhere God, I am learning to see an Everywhere Divine Presence.

This is the Presence Jesus revealed. Jesus was concerned about God with us in this world and about our giving the best possible expression to this Presence. His call to conversion is not about winning a place in heaven. It is not about winning forgiveness from a God who is withholding it. Rather, it is a passionate plea that we really see the Creative Divine Presence all around us, in all of us, here and now. It is a passionate plea that we use this seeing to transform our personal, social, religious, political, legal, educational, and economic interactions. As we see, so shall we—and the world—become.

FEBRUARY 28, 2012

4

Hold Fast to Hope, the Fragile Flowers Shout

Mary Lou Kownacki

I was typing a sentence condemning the brutal bombing of Iraqi children when she came into my study, pulled my chair from the desk, took my hand, and cried, "Hurry." We raced two blocks to an abandoned house where a front yard had just been attacked and overtaken by wild violets, by Johnny-jump-ups. We stood in silence for three long minutes and cheered the victory of beauty.

It is because I believe in the victory of beauty that I have walked in the annual Good Friday Pilgrimage for Peace sponsored by the Benedictine Sisters of Erie since 1980. By putting one foot in front of the other for seven miles, one can learn a lot about the journey from evil to beauty, darkness to light, despair to hope.

The pilgrimage begins in the inner city and winds its way to the monastery outside the city, stopping periodically to pray at stations where the body of Christ suffers today. We stop at the soup kitchen, where we are reminded that in the United States our city holds the dubious distinction of having the highest percentage of minority children living in poverty. There is a tavern that markets nude dancing, a symbol of how society encourages the exploitation and degradation of women.

Except for the prayers at the seven stations, the entire walk is done in silence. Parents with children, the lame in wheelchairs, the elderly, college students, and sisters—about 150 ordinary people—follow a simple wooden cross for the three-hour observance.

Once at the monastery, the pilgrims process into the chapel for the traditional Good Friday service with its readings, prayers, and adoration of the cross. After each pilgrim kisses the huge wooden cross and receives the broken body of Christ, the tabernacle door is closed, the altar is stripped, and silence returns. One could be left in despair, except that from the balcony comes the sound of a bell and two cantors sing over and over: "It is finished in beauty. It is finished in beauty." Then the final bell and the final silence.

Ah, yes, it is finished in beauty.

Tenacious wild violets erupting year after year no matter how many children are tortured worldwide is a glimmer of hope that God's plan for creation will triumph. Ordinary people participating in a seven-mile peace pilgrimage year after year despite growing lines at soup kitchens and escalating violence in our cities is a hope that death will not have the final word.

It is no mistake either, I believe, that Mary Magdalene first looked on the risen Jesus that early morning on the first day of the week, just after sunrise, and saw, of all things, a gardener. Our task is not about death, the empty tomb, and the empty shroud. It is about planting and sowing and caring for hope in whatever garden under the sun we find ourselves.

At the Easter Vigil in our monastery chapel a sister dances the Alleluia banner down the center aisle, accompanied by hand bells and a congregation of hundreds singing "Alleluia."

Two dozen people process down the side aisles carrying flowers of every color and fragrance. In less than a minute an empty sanctuary is transformed into an overpowering garden of lilacs and tulips and hyacinths and daffodils. Hold fast to hope, the fragile flowers shout.

Ah, yes, it is finished in beauty.

APRIL 7, 2017

✧ Sighting ✧

The Incredible Shrinking Man Sees It All

Did you ever see that wonderful black–and–white movie from the 1950s, "The Incredible Shrinking Man," written by Richard Matheson? The hero, Scott Carey, blond and tall, is sailing his boat in the ocean beneath an infinite sky. Suddenly a mist appears and covers him with radioactive dust. Slowly, he goes from six feet to three feet to three inches to infinitesimal.

At the end of the movie this dot of a man is walking in his garden through blades of grass that are taller than trees, among towering flowers that look like planets and suns, and sailing on a twig over a puddle as large as a lake. Suddenly, Carey *sees*. He is at home in the universe! Everything looks different, but God is everywhere. We hear his inner voice:

> *So close—the infinitesimal and the infinite. But suddenly,*
> *I knew they were really the two ends of the same concept.*
> *The unbelievably small and the unbelievably vast eventually*
> *meet—like the closing of a gigantic circle.*
>
> *I looked up, as if somehow I would grasp the heavens.*
> *The universe, worlds beyond number, God's silver tapestry*
> *spread across the night.*
>
> *And in that moment, I knew the answer to the riddle*
> *of the infinite. I had thought in terms of man's own limited*

dimension. I had presumed upon nature. That existence begins and ends is man's conception, not nature's. And I felt my body dwindling, melting, becoming nothing. My fears melted away. And in their place came acceptance. All this vast majesty of creation, it had to mean something. And then I meant something, too. Yes, smaller than the smallest, I meant something, too. To God, there is no zero. I still exist!

—MICHAEL LEACH

5

Every Month I Put a Poet in My Pocket

Pierre Eau Claire

John Adams (1735–1826), the second president of our country, held this conviction: "You will never be alone with a poet in your pocket." Could it that a good quantity of human loneliness is due to an absence of poetry, to the failure to put a poet in our pocket as we journey through this perilous life? And could it be that day in and day out they, these wordsmiths, these versifiers, are whispering to us pearls of wisdom and phrases that contain light and wisdom and humor?

Every month I put a poet in my pocket lest I become too afflicted with loneliness or get lost in the cosmos. They, those noble poets, point the way to some modicum of truth, goodness, and beauty. To them I owe a bundle of gratitude.

My January poet was the Belle of Amherst, Emily Dickinson. In her "If I Can Stop One Heart from Breaking" we find a whole philosophy (theology, if you will) of life:

being for others. Our lives will not be in vain if we offer that cup of cold water, offer others consolation, reach out to the hurting.

In February, Denise Levertov appeared with her "Primary Wonder." She confesses up front that too often she forgets the mystery of God's providential presence, distracted as she is by so many problems and worldly activities. But then, when the quiet comes, the mystery reemerges and she is filled with wonder and awe at what she sees with the eye of her soul.

Gerard Manley Hopkins is my March mentor. His "God's Grandeur" and that powerful phrase—"There lives the dearest freshness deep down things"—is one of the greatest lines in all of literature. And, of course, that deepest "deep down thing" is love, the heart of reality, the presence and gift of the brooding Holy Spirit.

April always brings e. e. cummings to mind and my second most favorite phrases in all of poetry: "the sweet small clumsy feet of April came / into the ragged meadow of my soul." For most of life I never knew that April had feet or that there was a ragged meadow in my soul. Now I know and rejoice in the fact.

In the merry month of May one can do no better than to invite Mary Oliver over for tea and have her recite "The Summer Day." Before leaving she will put a question upon you that is not rhetorical, a question about what you are planning to do with your life, so wild and so precious.

Then comes summer, a time to take a break from our busyness to smell the flowers and enjoy long, lazy summer days. Langston Hughes will tell you, in "A Negro Speaks of Rivers," how the Euphrates, Congo, Nile, and great Mississippi deepened his soul. The Carmelite Jessica Powers assures us in her "The House at Rest" that we gain our freedom through a virtuous life, enabling us to find blessedness and peace by way of good habits. Then, Dorothy Donnelley explains the magic of salt and of words, bringing savor and wit to our troubled human condition. "Domestic Magic" is a real treat.

September's poet, R. S. Thomas, takes us on a tour to the moor. If we are quiet we will experience God's presence in the wind and clean colors of that landscape. "The Moor" calls us to reverence and stillness. It also offers us unexpected graces, bread breaking and crumbling over us.

Our soul longs for peace. Where is it to be found? Wendell Berry, in his "The Peace of Wild Things," discovers it in God's creation, in the forest and ponds and stars. Autumn is a season rich in colors and beauty; autumn is a time to reconnect with nature and all the wild things of creation. We cannot afford to go through October without some verse.

Then there are the darkening days of November. Too easily we become lost and disoriented on this human journey. Is there some secret to help us find our way, or surprisingly, to be found? David Wagoner speaks powerfully of "standing still," of letting ourselves be found rather than hurrying and scurrying around in frantic circles. The secret is in the "here" and in the "now." "Lost" is a poem to pocket.

Every December I hurry back to my former teacher Gordon Gilsdorf, who not only instructed me in how to write but also in how to read poetry. More, he himself put pen to paper and wrote the poem "Lyrics for the Christian." The last stanza reads:

> I searched
> God's lexicon
> To fathom "Bethlehem"
> And "Calvary." It simply said:
> See "Love."

A poem in the pocket means we will be accompanied wherever we go.

MARCH 27, 2015

6

Poetry Is the Best Theology

Michael Leach

When I was in the seminary, our English teacher, Fr. Ignatius Burrill, introduced us to the poetry of Gerard Manley
Hopkins. I'll always remember these lines from "As King-
fishers Catch Fire":

> I say more: the just man justices;
> Keeps grace: that keeps all his goings
>   graces;
> Acts in God's eye what in God's eye he
>   is—
> Christ—for Christ plays in ten thou-
>   sand places,
> Lovely in limbs, and lovely in eyes not
>   his
> To the Father through the features of
>   men's faces.

When I was at home that summer, I glimpsed Christ
on Clark Street. I was walking down the street toward our

apartment near Wrigley Field and passed a down-and-out man leaning against a wall and drinking from a bottle in a paper bag. I recalled my friend Larry McCauley telling me about Ascension Church on nearby LaSalle Street with a crucified Jesus etched in stone on the wall. A legend under the cross reads, "Is it nothing to you who pass by?" I realized that the man on the street and the man on the cross were one.

I didn't know it then but Fr. Burrill and Larry McCauley had taught me that poetry is the best theology.

Poetry evokes what is good, beautiful, and true. It imagines the unimaginable, describes the indefinable, and unveils what our senses cannot know or our intellect figure out. Poetry is theology leaping out of the file cabinet and into the heart. It is the Word or words that stir our souls.

And, paradoxically, you don't have to put words to paper to be a poet. Jesus never wrote a poem. The only words he ever wrote were on the sand. And the rain washed those away. His life was poetry. He was the Word made flesh.

A poet is a poet because, like Jesus, a poet sees what is really there. Jesus saw goodness in the adulteress, wholeness in the leper, forgiveness in the thief on the cross. He even beheld innocence behind the masks of those who taunted, scourged, and crucified him. Jesus acted in God's eye what in God's eye he was. When asked who he was and how he healed, Jesus told his disciples, "Come and *see*."

A poet is a seer who cultivates the Christlike faculty of looking at what is temporal and discerning what is eternal. As Jesus saw splendor in the lilies of the field, the poet, too, perceives power in everyday places. Poet William Carlos Williams understood that everything depends on "a red wheel barrow glazed with rain water near the white chickens."

A poet also divines the Divine in the most unlikely places. J. D. Salinger's alter ego Buddy Glass talked about his poet brother Seymour (See More) who "had a distracting habit, most of his adult life, of investigating loaded ashtrays with his index finger, clearing all the cigarette ends to the sides—smiling from ear to ear as he did it—as if he expected to see Christ himself curled up cherubically in the middle, and he never looked disappointed."

It was Buddy who urged his sister Franny, an aspiring actress, to "act for God," and brought her back from the brink of a breakdown by reminding her always to act for the Fat Lady in the back row, assuring her: "There isn't anyone anywhere who isn't Seymour's Fat Lady. Don't you know that? Don't you know that goddam secret yet? And don't you know—listen to me, now—don't you know who that Fat Lady really is? . . . Ah, buddy. Ah, buddy. It's Christ Himself. Christ Himself, buddy."

Jesus put it straight: "I was hungry, and you fed me. I was thirsty, and you gave me a drink. I was a stranger, and you invited me into your home. I was naked, and you gave me clothing. I was sick, and you cared for me. I was in prison, and you visited me. I tell you the truth, whenever you did this to one of the least of these my brothers and sisters, you were doing it to me!"

That is poetry. That is theology. That is real.

The poet sees: Christ on Clark Street; Christ in the back row; Christ nearer than breathing, closer than hands and feet. "What is essential," wrote Antoine de Saint-Exupéry, "is invisible to the eye." Jesus invites us: "Come and *see*."

MARCH 28, 2014

7

How to Take a Soul Picture

Joyce Rupp

Several weeks ago I made a trip to Kansas to visit a friend who has lung cancer. We had little contact with each other for a number of years, and I sensed our visit would be a special one. Little did I know how special. When I arrived in Topeka I learned that Ken's wife, Bibi, had taken him to the E.R. that morning because of severe chest pains. I rushed to the hospital, hoping we could have some quality time together. Indeed, we did. I found Ken to be as I remembered: gentle, optimistic, loving, and faith filled. Fortunately he had not lost his sly sense of humor either.

When I was readying to say goodbye, Ken asked if he could take a picture of me and would I stand at the foot of his bed. Being a bit puzzled (knowing he had no camera), I proceeded to do so. "There," he chuckled, "just perfect." Then he asked me if I would stand there quietly for a minute. As I did so, Ken gazed at my face with a soft smile. In turn, I gazed back at him. That's how we "took photos" of one another.

As I looked in silence at Ken's face, my gaze moved to focus on his eyes. It was as if I could enter the light there and see far beyond his physical being to a sphere of pure love. When the minute was over and Ken thanked me, I responded, "I'm awed. I think there was a moment when I saw your soul." I know he understood.

After I returned home I sent Ken a note and affirmed his beautiful approach to remembering a friend. Here is the email I received in return: "I got out of the hospital on Saturday and every now and then I take your picture out and look at it. I did not wear it out though and I cannot lose it. I can look at it anytime, even in the dentist chair, and he never says a word. He just keeps drilling."

Later that week Ken sent me another note when I asked him if I could share his "taking a picture" with my readers: "Sure, Joyce, you can use that simple little picture thing. It's easy. Flowers are great subjects. Just take a time exposure in your mind. Close your eyes. Review your picture with the real subject and it is secured. Once in a while you can take out your album for review. And at night you can get lots of memories, laughs, and good times. Human subjects are best. It has to be a time exposure, though, or it doesn't work. No copyright rules apply. Oh, I forgot. Beginners should avoid time exposures of wild beasts, advancing tornadoes, and spiders."

One day as I was taking out my "photo" of Ken, I recalled a section in John O'Donohue's *Anam Cara* where he describes the human face as "an artistic achievement." The Irish poet goes on to write: "On such a small surface an incredible variety and intensity of presence can be expressed. . . . There is always a special variation of presence in each one. Each face is a particular intensity of human presence. . . . When you return again and see the face you love, at this moment you enjoy a feast of seeing. In that face, you see the intensity and depth of loving presence looking towards you and meeting you."

Since being with Ken, I am taking more soul pictures of those I care about. I'm relishing my growing photo album. It truly is a feast of seeing. May it be so for you as well.

JULY 6, 2012

8

Facebook Can Be a Conduit of Grace

James Martin

It's easy to make fun of Facebook. It gobbles up time and takes us away from our work. It encourages us to post inane photos (I'm not immune to this temptation), for example, what's on our plate at Applebee's ("Mmm, baby back ribs!"). It invites people to boast of their accomplishments or popularity. ("Can't believe ten people showed up for my autograph party!") It fosters navel-gazing, solipsism, and even hypochondria. ("Sore throat *again*.")

Worst of all, it takes us away from one-on-one contact with live human beings and substitutes virtual relationships for lasting ones. That's the most damning critique of Facebook. Rather than posting a happy birthday message on a person's wall (which I do almost every day—though not for the same person), it's probably better to call the person up. Five minutes of real time is better than an hour of Facebook time.

The other night a friend noticed that I had just posted a comment on his page, and he called me.

"I figured you'd like to talk with me in person," he joked.

"Oh, I can't talk to you now," I joked back. "I'm too busy posting on your page!"

But like many other social media sites, and more broadly the Web itself, Facebook can also be a conduit of grace. Surprised? Of course not. You know that God can work through any medium, even ones that are supposedly tearing us apart. The easiest way to illustrate this is with a story.

A few months ago I noticed a Facebook page for alumni of the Ridge Park Elementary School in Conshohocken, Pennsylvania, of which I myself am a proud alumnus. And the other day one of my childhood friends posted a handful of color photos that I had not only never before seen, but that showed something that I had entirely forgotten.

Snapped on a field behind our school, clearly during recess, the photos show my friends and me in the process of building a human pyramid. The first snapshot depicts us readying the pyramid; the second the triumphant success; the third, our tumbling over one another as the pyramid collapsed. The photos were taken on what must have been a cool day in early fall or late spring, since some of us are wearing lightweight jackets, while others are in short sleeves. I would guess that it was the fifth grade.

I can't describe how moving it was to see these photos. It was as if God were giving my soul a window into a day that I had long forgotten. I felt like a time traveler as I stared at those images, taking in all the details. With a start, I even remembered the pants I was wearing: blue-and-green-striped bell bottoms—way cool in 1968!

What shocked me most was this: Each photo showed me with a huge smile on my face. What a blessing to be reminded of this moment that I had utterly forgotten.

God is with us all the days of our lives, blessing us with friends, touching us with warm and funny moments, accompanying us throughout our hours. But many of these moments are so fleeting, so evanescent, and seemingly so unimportant that we don't remember them at all. I'll bet that on that day in the fifth grade, all we did after recess was talk about our pyramid: how we had always wanted to do it, how much fun it was, and how we laughed when we all fell on top of one another. Maybe I remembered it for a few days. Then I forgot it. For forty years.

The photos got me thinking about the other graced moments that we can forget. God is always looking out for us, in our struggles as we try to build something, in our triumph as we sit atop the pile, and in our failures as we collapse on ourselves. God is always aware of us, always giving us light. But we're not always aware of God. And sometimes, even if we are, we forget it immediately afterward.

So the photos were a surprise. Even more surprising, they came from a supposedly shallow social media site. God is at work at all times. And everywhere.

Even on Facebook.

9

Love Shines through Our Evolving Faces

Joni Woelfel

I see your true colors shining through.
—Cindy Lauper

It's been eighteen years since my face became paralyzed following surgery for Meniere's disease, an inner ear disorder that can drive you mad. I was at the end of my rope with relentless vertigo, hearing loss, tinnitus, and incapacitating imbalance. I signed a release acknowledging the surgery's risk. Something did go wrong, and I was left with permanent Bell's palsy on the left side of my face. It droops like melting wax.

My surgeon wrote me a caring letter about how when we have no shoes we should think of the person who has no feet. I respected the cliche and looked for its truth. Over and over in my life I have seen the wisdom of this perspective. I generally avoid comparisons, but when I view stories about people who have facial neurofibromatosis with painful, horrendous tumors that cover their entire face, my heart breaks for them and my condition pales. I learn what it means to behold a person's true colors.

Mother Teresa wrote that "seeking the face of God in everything, everyone, all the time" is what it means to be "contemplative in the heart of the world." Victor Hugo in *Les Miserables* said that "to love another person is to see the face of God." It is a blessing to see and comprehend what we so often quote. Many people do, and they inspire us.

Years ago when my three sons first saw my distorted face, I was anxious about how they would take it. They were stunned for a moment, and then my sweet youngest blurted out, "Mom, you look like the Joker from Batman!" We all laughed and that was that. Now, having integrated the fact that how I look is just who I am, I rarely even think about it when we are together. Friends, relatives, and family have been wonderful, reminding me of author Toni Morrison's powerful words about how our faces should light up when a child (or loved one) enters the room.

I am still self-conscious and guarded about my crooked face when I encounter strangers, such as clerks, receptionists, waiters, and waitresses. But I have never had a bad experience. Rather, they tend to be more solicitous, which causes me to realize how many compassionate people there are in the world. I am grateful to these hardworking people who are simply nice human beings. To me, having good manners is a sign of a person's professionalism, integrity, good will, and maturity.

Now I sometimes wish I could write a letter to the world about the pitfalls of superficiality and vanity. Advertisements that herald external beauty as the most important aspect of a person's worth are troubling. Our culture's obsession with looks, ageless beauty, and the repulsion of any facial irregularity can become a form of spiritual paralysis, a narcissistic perspective that impedes depth, growth, and the true meaning of joy and service. Granted, we all like to feel good about ourselves, and there is nothing wrong with enjoying being attractive and putting our best face forward—but to judge others or ourselves solely by how we look is a shallow, unbalanced approach to self worth. After all, our evolving faces are road maps that reflect where life has taken us.

Recently my ninety-six year old Aunt Minnie, my cousin Roger, two sisters, Julie and Karen, and I piled into my brother Scott's pickup for a tour of his RV park. I happened to catch a glimpse of my crooked, paralyzed face in the rearview mirror, and feeling a pang of discontent, thought, in my colorful Minnesota language, "Darn it, I look like heck." Then, admiring my red plaid jacket and lipstick, I thought, "Oh well," and brought my attention back to the joy of being with my family. It was a wonderful day. Later when I saw photos I was reminded of Cyndi Lauper's song *True Colors* and how love can shine through whatever challenges we experience.

One of my favorite experiences of seeing with the eye of the soul was when Aunt Minnie (who is legally blind and can't see me) gave me a hug and said with such heartfelt sincerity, "You look beautiful!" To me this is how God sees all of us, with blind eyes that see only what is real. "Beauty is not in the face," wrote Kahil Gibran, "beauty is a light in the heart."

✧ SIGHTING ✧

Thomas Merton Stands on the Corner

In Louisville, at the corner of Fourth and Walnut, in the center of the shopping district, I was suddenly overwhelmed with the realization that I loved all these people, that they were mine and I theirs, that we could not be alien to one another even though we were total strangers. It was like waking from a dream of separateness, of spurious self-isolation in a special world. . . .

This sense of liberation from an illusory difference was such a relief and such a joy to me that I almost laughed out loud. . . . I have the immense joy of being man, a member of a race in which God Himself became incarnate. As if the sorrows and stupidities of the human condition could overwhelm me, now that I realize what we all are. And if only everybody could realize this! But it cannot be explained. There is no way of telling people that they are all walking around shining like the sun.

Then it was as if I suddenly saw the secret beauty of their hearts, the depths of their hearts where neither sin nor desire nor self-knowledge can reach, the core of their reality, the person that each one is in God's eyes. If only they could all see themselves as they really are. If only we could see each other that way all the time. There would be no more war, no more hatred, no more cruelty, no more greed. . . . But this cannot be seen, only believed and "understood" by a peculiar gift.

—THOMAS MERTON,
CONJECTURES OF A GUILTY BYSTANDER

10

My Days with the Other Old Yoga Ladies

Sidney Callahan

Something unexpected is happening to me in this spring's senior center yoga classes. Something over and above the shock of finding myself at seventy-nine in the "old–old" category. There's no denying it: I was born in 1933, the year Hitler took power, the banks closed, and President Roosevelt declared that "the only thing we have to fear is fear itself."

Who could have imagined that someday we'd all be living so much longer?

In the fifty years Dan and I have lived in our New York river town on the Hudson, far fewer children play in the streets but many more gray heads fill the aisles of the A & P, the church pews, and the library tables.

Our spanking new community center offers daily senior activities and services. Besides yoga there is tai chi, line dancing, aerobics, computer classes, swimming, shopping, lectures, luncheons, and regular holiday celebrations.

Unexpectedly, as a member of the aging exercise scene, I am having the novel experience of becoming attracted to the beauty of old women's bodies.

Instead of feeling dread and revulsion toward aging flesh as the fashionable media have it, my response has grown positive and pleasant. How natural and endearing it seems to have loose padding on upper arms, necks, middles, and behinds. Perhaps a harbinger of my changing perspective was sounded several years ago when my grandson asked what those flopping things on my upper arms were, and I shot back, "That's excess wisdom, Liam."

By now the crinkles, creases, brown spots, and moles on bodies advertise character. It's just as lovely to be filled out, veiny, or boney as it is to be fit, toned, or strong. That worn and well-used look has charms.

My appreciative range for bodies has extended far beyond my habitual baby worship. Who can resist plump little hands and feet, miniature ears, big eyes, and rounded foreheads? Our delight in babies arises from the promise of their future. With an aging woman's body, it is the marks of past living that appeal. Engraved on the faces, figures, and hands are decades of experiences undergone.

Think here of the aesthetic appeal of old houses and antique silver and furniture. A distressed finish and a well-rubbed patina attract our eyes. Fading flowers and autumn leaves manifest beauty. Trees filled with moss or gnarled by winds express variety. On the Maine coast we wonder at earth's history in the eroded rocks.

The old bodies of women at the senior center bear witness to fulsome long-term use. Their flesh is imprinted with a lifetime of loving care; sex and childbirth, mothering and grandmothering, nurturing the ill and coping with loss have left their traces. When I look at their hands I think of the decades of cooking, cleaning, celebrating, and enabling work for their families and community. A large part of this generation was engaged in homemaking rather than full-time careers. But who knows? Retired PhDs don't look different from anyone else.

I wonder if these other yoga ladies are as surprised as I am by becoming so old. Since my self feels the same as it ever did, I'm often startled by looking in a mirror or seeing the gray hair of my spouse, friends, and middle-aged sons. My adult children's friends are beginning to look old!

It's so odd to have lived so long as my body has been constantly changing. The "I" is the same, but the bodily me grows different. My body is past time and experience made visible. There's that childhood scar, those stretch marks, the trace of operations, loosened muscles, capped teeth—along with laugh lines (and cry lines) galore.

The embodied person living through time is a mystery of mysteries. Our ever changing, not so solid flesh speeds ever faster through time, but toward what? Our faith says that our embodied selves are on the way to a new more abundant life of joy with God. Our life on earth is a fireworks display flaming up into invisibility. The hope that sustains us is that new birth is coming. It is *right* to affirm that the marks of aging are a good and holy sight.

Old age is bringing me ever more gratitude. And my weekdays with the old yoga ladies are teaching me two truths. Delight, not disgust, is the divine Creator's way with bodies. And just as true, God is a God of surprises.

JUNE 8, 2012

11

Praying with the Eye of the Soul

Kathy Coffey

Soul seeing reminds me of a visit to the eye doctor. She tries various lenses with different degrees of fuzziness until one finally reaches clarity. "That's it!" we say in delight. Suddenly, we can see. If we look through the right spiritual lens, we may also recognize times of prayer where we hadn't noticed them before. Some prayerful moments are as dramatic as bounding across a stage, others as humble as laundry. The common denominator is the spirit of the Creator stirring within us and our response to that voice. Here are people fully engaged with their lives and praying with the eye of the soul:

- The husband who watches beside the hospital bed of his wife. He says nothing. He holds her hand as he has for the past two weeks.
- The mother who rises to nurse the baby for the third time that night. With half-opened eyes she bumbles

toward the crib, scoops up the infant, and feeds him sleepily.

- The student who completes a week of final exams, three term papers, a group project, and the organization of a canned-food drive. He dives into bed but pauses for a moment before falling asleep. Words addressed to the mysterious Holy One come muffled by exhaustion: "Thanks. I got it all done."

- The business executive who knows that a long day looms ahead. She faces the window and lifts both hands in an eloquent gesture. "Thank you for a new day," her hands seem to say. "I am yours, O God. Help me to be kind as well as efficient."

- The two friends who meet over coffee to talk through a dilemma that concerns them both. They listen carefully, lean across the table toward each other, joke, and respect each other's truth. They leave knowing clearly what action they must take; the caffeine was in the conversation.

- The protester who takes a deep breath and steps across the line at the nuclear weapons plant, thinking: "If I go to jail, I go to jail. But I can't let conscience lie down and die."

- The artist who launches a new project, excited about its potential while still aware that it will take many long hours to complete. Still, a tantalizing intrigue hovers over the beginning. How will this look when it's finished? What will emerge?

- The older sister who knows it's drudgery, but does it anyway. "Just this once, Sam," she tells her younger brother. "I'll throw your jeans in the wash with my dark load so you'll have clean ones for the party." They grin at each other in the easy camaraderie of people who know they'll fall again, and once again, they'll bail each other out.

Do you recognize yourself in any of these moments of prayer? These are not the long, uninterrupted stretches with books and formal words that many associate with prayer. Instead, they accord with Jacob's surprise: "Surely the Lord is in this place—and I did not know it!" (Gen 28:16). Or, as Dorothy Day once asked, "Since when are words the only acceptable form of prayer?"

In reflection after or during the events mentioned above, these folks may recognize God's presence there. God is delighting in them. And they resonate with God's dream for them, becoming wiser, more generous, bold, creative, active, or contemplative—whatever God desired at their creation. So they consecrate their actions to God who is everywhere. An attitude of prayer requires two parts, like two hands clapping or two wings beating. Bringing God into daily life means a constant movement back and forth between action and reflection.

Surely this rhythm marked Jesus's days on earth. He never said, "Today I multiplied loaves and fishes, I don't need to pray." Instead, he entered solitude to be with God. His prayer fueled his ministry and deepened his compassion.

Prayer is larger than any formula, holding a splendid range of possibilities. The God who creates unique fingerprints, snowflakes, and over a million kinds of insects must love variety. God relishes all the different voices of God's children, no matter how bumbling they may sound. Furthermore, God starts the conversation, coming to us in a myriad of ways tailored specifically to the individual. Some may find God more in events, like liturgy or healthcare; others in people or inspiring places where nature is saturated with God's affection or in nurturing things: flowers, stained glass, hot coffee. The human response is sensitivity to God's initiative, alertness to God's activity. Praying with the eye of the soul is simply responding to God's grace in our lives moment by moment, what Jesus meant by "praying always." As many spiritual writers say, the only way to fail at prayer is to not show up.

JANUARY 20, 2012

12

We Hear God with the Same Ear God Hears Us

Michael Leach

> *Be still and know that I am God!*
> —PSALM 46:11

Growing up Catholic nobody taught me to listen to God. Parents and teachers taught me to talk to God. They said prayer was praising God, telling him you love him or you're sorry, asking God for something and then thanking him whether you got it or not. The only person who suggested that prayer was listening to God was my Uncle Barney, who was a Protestant, and I didn't pay attention to him because he was Protestant—what did he know?

In the seminary our spiritual directors taught us about meditation and contemplation, the latter a gift of wordless prayer reserved for mystics and saints whose palms bleed, so forget about it. They trained us to meditate by thinking about a scripture or imagining ourselves in Jesus's time, but they never taught us to be still and experience the love of God that's here and now. Our first spiritual director, Fr. Skippy Krost, was a contemporary of St. Ignatius. (He dragged his right leg as he swept down the aisle of the chapel each night, and thus in their charity generations of seminarians had dubbed him Skippy.) I dreaded when Skippy would have us close our eyes and clench our foreheads into fists and imagine looking up at the foot of the cross with all our might. The purpose was to feel Jesus's blood falling on our heads and burning our eyes, reminding us of how much we made him suffer for our sins. That was one of our meditations before trying to go to sleep.

Fortunately, once a year we had a five-day silent Ignatian retreat. How peaceful it was to walk around the lake with the encouragement to "listen for God" and "find God in all things." Suddenly, the monkey brain would stop chattering and we'd stop in our tracks and know what the poet Gerard Manley Hopkins knew: "The world is charged with the grandeur of God." Somehow, if only for a moment, everything was where it was supposed to be. It was moments like that that stanched the bleeding.

Vinita Hampton Wright in her book *Days of Deepening Friendship* encourages everyone to "spend a few moments each day quietly listening for God. Don't say anything or ask for anything. Or if you do ask for something, may it be, 'God, help me tune in to your voice.'"

It's taken me a lifetime to appreciate that prayer is not about pretending to be in the past or asking about the future but about being awake and aware in the presence of God. Slowly, yearly, through a little bit of wisdom and a lot of suffering, I am coming to realize that the most beneficial prayer is listening.

Listening to "the still, small voice" that is "not in the wind, not in the earthquake, and not in the fire" (1 Kings 19:11–12) but in our very being.

God is talking to us all the time, but we're either too busy talking to God or obsessing on our own thoughts to have "ears to hear" God's soothing voice (Mark 4:9). I have spent a major portion of my life thinking about what other people are thinking about me, and feeling guilty about anything related to being alive. And all that time God has been saying to me, gently, softly, persistently, "I don't want to kill you. I want to heal you, give you peace, assurance and joy."

When I meditate now, here is how I meditate: I sit straight and watch my thoughts without evaluating them. I can do that for up to two seconds at a time now. So when that falls apart, I just ask God a question and listen for the answer. The question I ask the most is, "What do you want me to know, God?" And the answer is invariably the same: "I am here for you."

If "we see God with the same eye that God sees us," as the mystic Meister Eckhart says, then it must be also true that we hear God with the same ear God hears us.

"I am here for you!"

God is here for me, and I am here for God. It's like walking around St. Mary's Lake all over again.

✧ SIGHTING ✧

A View from the Kitchen

God walks among the pots and pans.
— St. Thérèse of Lisieux

13

Life Is Headed Somewhere Good

Richard Rohr

Advent—from the Latin for "a coming, an approach, or an arrival"—is upon us. This season is more than a sentimental, reminiscent waiting for a new baby Jesus. The need for adult Christianity and Jesus's actual message is so urgent that we cannot allow the great feast of Christmas and its preparation in Advent to be watered down in any way. The suffering, injustice, and devastation on this planet are too great to settle for an infantile gospel or Jesus. Jesus taught that the "reign of God" or the "kingdom of God" asks a great deal of us personally—surrender, simplicity, solidarity with suffering.

Advent is a time to focus our anticipation on the eternal and cosmic Christ, beyond and before the child in the manger. Jesus is the microcosmic expression of the macrocosm, the union of human and divine, psychic and physical, in a single life and person. The Christ includes and goes further than Jesus, beyond space and time. Jesus is a concrete and personal embodiment of universal Love. Christ is the blueprint and icon of God's loving presence and plan—always and everywhere. It is to this adult and cosmic Christ that we say, "Come, Lord Jesus" (Rev 22:20).

The creation poem in the first chapter of Genesis portrays a joyful, creative outpouring of Love. The Big Bang is really the first moment of incarnation in our universe, before Jesus even took on human flesh. God takes shape in color, movement, form, and texture—incarnate and present in each living thing. From the moment of our universe's inception, along the slow stages of evolution, and through the life, death, and resurrection of Jesus, we see that life is headed somewhere good. We can trust that death simply brings new forms of Love making itself known.

Thus, ever since, Christ has "come again"—and again and again—in every created thing, drawing creation toward greater wholeness, fullness, and union.

> And the Word [or Blueprint] became flesh, and dwelt among us, and we saw his glory, the glory as of the only begotten from the Father, full of grace and truth. . . . For of his fullness we all received grace upon grace. (John 1:14, 16)

The mystery of Christ is revealed whenever you are able to see the psychic and the physical coexisting, in any moment, in any event, and in any person. God's hope for history seems to be that humanity will one day be able to recognize its own dignity as the divine dwelling place, which it also shares with the rest of creation. (If we cannot honor our own human dignity, how could we possibly recognize and honor the inherent dignity of warblers, winter wheat, or water?)

God creates things that create themselves, and we are called to be co-creators with God (Rom 8:28). Rather than Jesus coming to fulfill us, we have come to fulfill the cosmic Christ (Col 1:17–20, 24). Evolution, the idea that something is unfolding and coming to a fullness is an active, ongoing process. We are all a part of this movement of the ever-growing cosmic Christ that is coming to be in this one great act of giving birth (Rom 8:22).

I don't know when it will happen or what it will look like to reach the tipping point, for the Christ mystery to come to fullness. All I know is that this meaning, planted in the middle of things, gives us *direction, purpose, hope,* and *confidence.*

We're still living in the in-between, slowly edging forward, with much resistance and push back. Creation is "groaning in anticipation . . . standing on tiptoe waiting for the revelation of the sons and daughters of God" (Rom 8:22–23). Evolution is never a straight path, but three steps forward and two steps back, as we see throughout scripture, history, nature, and in our own lives. We fight change and death to our small selves; we avoid uncertainty and the unknown. Yet the descent into darkness is necessary to all life, to transformation, and to fresh expressions of God. Creation begins with the Spirit hovering over a formless, dark deep to bring forth light and life.

When we demand any completion to history on our terms, when we demand that our anxiety or any dissatisfaction be taken away, saying as it were, "Why did life let me down? Why didn't I get what I wanted or expected?" we are refusing to say, "Come, Lord Jesus." We are refusing to hold out for the *full story*.

Foundational hope demands a foundational belief in a world that is still and always unfolding. To stay on the ride, to trust the trajectory, to know it is moving, and moving somewhere always better, is just another way to describe faith. Evolutionary thinking is actually contemplative thinking because it leaves the full field of the future in God's hands and agrees to humbly hold the present. Evolutionary thinking allows both knowing and not knowing, at the same time.

"Come, Lord Jesus," the Advent mantra, means that all of history must live from a kind of deliberate emptiness, a chosen non-fulfillment. Perfect fullness is always yet to come; we do not need to demand it now. This keeps the field of life wide open to grace and to a future created by God through our surrender and creative participation. This is what it means to be *awake*, what it means to be in Advent—aware, alive, attentive, alert, anticipating. Advent is, above all else, a call to full consciousness and a forewarning about the high price of consciousness.

"Come, Lord Jesus" is a leap into the kind of freedom and surrender that is rightly called the virtue of hope: the patient and trustful willingness to live without closure, without resolution, and still be content and even happy because our Satisfaction is now at another level, and our Source is beyond ourselves. We are able to trust that Christ *will* come again, just as Jesus has come into our past, into our private dilemmas, and into our suffering world. Our past then becomes our prologue, and "Come, Lord Jesus" is not a cry of desperation but an assured shout of cosmic hope.

This is the good news the angels gave Mary and the shepherds in a very specific and concrete way. We can now trust that history—and our small roles within the larger story—is moving in a positive direction. We who know the end from the beginning, who trust the Christ mystery, must participate in the movement toward the fullness of every living thing's union in Love. We *are* the Second Coming of Christ!

December 1, 2017

14

Have a Defiant Christmas!

John Shea

Sprawl

In those long ago days of Christmas innocence when it always snowed gently in a starry and windless night, my parents would hustle my sisters and me into the back seat of the car. We would drive slowly, snow crunching under cold tires, into the neighborhoods of the rich to see the lights.

The lights were decorations that people put up on the outside of their houses and lawns. Multicolored lights would be strung over an entire house, etching door frames and windows, wrapped round into wreaths and bows. In the frozen front yard there were figures of cardboard and plastic, even stone, ranging in size from a small child to an overgrown adult. They were the usual suspects, a mix of *The Night before Christmas* and the crib—reindeer and wise men, sleighs and shepherds, elves and Mary, angels and carolers, Santa Claus and Baby Jesus. Occasionally, the stiff, on-guard soldiers from the *Nutcracker Suite* would make an appearance. All were lit up so that night passengers in slow-moving cars could gawk through frosted windows and say, "Look at that one!"

But it was not these sprawling scenes that first welcomed me into the truth of Christmas.

Contrast

One Christmas when we returned from our trip to see the lights, I pushed out of the back seat, straightened up, and saw our house. We lived in a two flat. My grandparents lived on the first floor, and since they usually went to bed around nine (a practice I have recently begun to understand), their flat was dark. Our flat on the second floor was also dark—except for the Christmas tree.

The tree was strung with lights, and their soft glow could be seen through the upper window. The outer darkness was all around, yet the tree shone in the darkness. There was no razzle-dazzle, no blinking on and off, no glitz, no "Oh, wow!" There was just a steady shining, a simple juxtaposition of light and darkness. Its beauty drew me.

I ran up the stairs. My parents had already unlocked the door and turned on the house lights. I sat in a chair and stayed with the tree. The attraction of the tree continued for a while and then began to recede. Soon the practical took over. I noticed some tinsel that needed to be smoothed and re-hung. As I tinkered with it, whatever was left of the tree's radiance dimmed. Then, abruptly, the revelation ceased. It became merely a pine tree shedding needles on the rug.

It was only when I was older that I reflected on what my child's heart had intuited. Christmas celebrates an inner light, a tree of lights inside the house of our being, and invites us to come close and ponder its beauty. We notice this light because it is contrasted with an outer darkness. Although the outer darkness does not go away, the inner light defies this darkness, refusing to allow it to dictate the terms of existence. "What has come into being *in* him was life and the life was the light of all people. The light shines in the darkness, and the darkness did not overcome it" (John 1:4–5).

Defiance

The Christmas revelation can be phrased this way: no matter how severe the darkness of the outer world is, it cannot overcome the inner and transcendent light. Give the darkness its due but not your soul. Although we do not always reflect on it, there is an edge to Christmas, an in-your-face attitude. Chesterton put it simply and well: "A religion that defies the world should have a feast that defies the weather." So I wish everyone a defiant Christmas.

Of course, I really want everyone to have what the Christmas cards say—unvarnished peace, love, and joy. But that is not what we always get. Christmas arrives to find our health precarious; our careers, jobs, or vocations under stress; our finances dipping badly; our relationships in need of repair; our society and world either slightly or wildly insane, threatening us in ways we never imagined.

We need to push back. When the outer world is darkness, we need to find and rest in the inner world of light and bring that light into the intimidating darkness. Since this inner world is rooted in a transcendent love, it is more powerful than all the attacks that emerge from both our finitude and sin. When we bring it forth, we walk the path of gentle defiance. We are neither negative nor angry. We have just managed to find a greater love by which to be held and energized. This capacity for defiance may be the Christmas gift that we will all need to unwrap during one December or another.

DECEMBER 19, 2014

15

I Could Use a Transfiguration

Michael Leach

It's 7:30 a.m. I look in the mirror and see the face of Tommy Lee Jones in the last scene of *Lincoln*. My wrinkly bald head looks like a cracked egg. Bags slump under my eyes and roll across my cheeks like the Himalayas. Where did it go? Was it ever there? No matter.

I droop back into the bedroom and look at Vickie lying on her back like a mummy, her hands crossed over her chest. She looks like Boris Karloff. I don't care.

I pick up the July issue of *Give Us This Day* from the nightstand and take it with me to the rocking chair by the window. It's a sunny morning but my head is cloudy. I sit down and open the monthly. It's time for some inspiration. An epiphany perhaps. A transfiguration. I could use one.

Today's reading is about the burning bush. I've always liked that one. First it's just a bush. Then it's fire. God fills Moses's mind with light. Reminds me of the time Thomas Merton was standing on a street corner in downtown Louisville and the light of a transfiguration blew him away. All of a sudden Louisville wasn't Louisville anymore. The city glowed. "There is no way of telling people," he said, "that they are walking around shining like the sun. There are no strangers. The gate of heaven is everywhere."

In the movie *Field of Dreams* the ghost of his father asks the hero, Ray Kinsella, "Is this heaven?"

"No," he says. "It's Iowa."

Ray reminds me of the Zen seeker to whom mountains were always mountains and rivers always rivers until one day a transfiguration hits him and mountains are no longer mountains and river no longer rivers. His epiphany doesn't last though, and once again mountains are mountains and rivers rivers. But he is never the same again.

Iowa. Heaven. Iowa.

That must have been the apostles' experience when they climbed the mountain with Jesus and all of a sudden Jesus was no longer Jesus and his whole appearance changed and his clothes blazed like lightning and Moses and Elijah appeared next to him in splendor. The disciples had been sleepy but now they were awake, and Peter said, "Lord, it is good for us to be here! We're going to build shrines for you and Moses and Elijah!" The Bible then says, "Peter didn't know what he was talking about." So like us. He was trying to capture the experience and it was like trying to grab the wings of a butterfly that lands on your shoulder and watching it fly away. A cloud covers the mountain and it's all over. But Peter would never be the same.

I think of moments in my life when mountains were no longer mountains and rivers no longer rivers. Standing on the corner of Central Park West and 72nd Street waiting for a bus after seeing my shrink and hearing, really hearing for the first time, that I didn't have to get people to like me, I was God's special child, and then seeing, really seeing, peace in the midst of chaos, harmony in one bus going this way, another that, beauty in a cup of coffee spilled along the curb, love appearing as everyone everywhere. I was silent with gratitude. It was a moment not unlike that Merton or Peter experienced. One of those moments when you can see the veins on the leaves of trees a block away, and all the planets and all the people and all the squirrels are just where they're supposed to be. Transfigurations don't happen on mountains or street corners. They happen in us. I've never seen Central Park that way again, but I've never been the same again either.

I think of less dramatic transfigurations in my life: sitting with a group of old people whose memories are few and realizing that God sees each of them as he created them, as his perfect child; or sitting in my rocker reading a spiritual book and my eyes get wide and I know what I need to know without needing words. The book drops from my hands and I am at peace. At least for a while.

I wish I could have one of those moments now. *Give Us This Day* is still in my hands.

I'd like to be like the Zen fishmonger who after his transfiguration still peddled fish and still smelled of fish, but who when his friends asked, "What's so great about your life now?" answered, "Well, everything is exactly the same as it was before, except that now wherever I go the dead trees come to life."

I look out the window at what might be an emerald forest but see only the same old trees. I'm still the Zen seeker for whom mountains again are mountains and rivers rivers. So it goes.

I get up and lay the book on the nightstand. Vickie is awake and she sees my face and smiles. Boris Karloff never looked so good.

JULY 31, 2015

16

Light Touches My Soul
Forty Years Later

Tom Smith

I slid into the fourth pew from the back on the left side of Dahlgren chapel at Georgetown University. It was a 1975 summer evening with a soft sun backlighting the five paneled stained-glass window featuring the Sacred Heart of Jesus behind the altar. It was quiet, a solemn quiet. I was on my knees and then, in a slow moving but eerie transition, I was no longer in the fourth pew from the back on the left side of the chapel in Georgetown University.

I didn't know where I was, but I felt a light touching my soul. It was peaceful, stirring, fully engaging, and warm with a gentle tingle that I knew was massaging my spirit. I felt the light absorb me and infuse me with acceptance and verification, words that do not do justice to the experience but are still minimally accurate. Much later I connected the light with the descriptions by people who have had near-death experiences. I heard nothing distinct that I can remember but I heard the presence, if that makes any sense.

It took about an hour for things to get back to normal. Of course, normal was never the same again, even though I tried to act like it was for decades. It was an experience that I locked up in my mental safe-deposit box and only took out rarely when I had the courage to ask God to provide the second matching key to open the box. Every time I glanced at it I didn't know what to do, so I quickly put it back.

I don't know how long the experience lasted (maybe ten minutes?) because when I was aware again that I was in the fourth pew from the back on the left side of the Georgetown chapel, I just sat there stunned. The mellow glow remained but I had no idea what had just happened. I still don't know but now, forty years later, I am willing and more prepared spiritually and emotionally to open that safe-deposit box and spend more time in the presence of that Event. I was always aware that it was personal, relational, and that it didn't just happen *to* me but also *with* me. I was not a spectator but a deeply involved participant even though the Mystery was clearly the Initiator and a lot bigger than me.

Fran and I were at Georgetown for a two-week scripture course. When it ended, she went home and I stayed another week to edit a booklet for the National Catholic Education Association. That's when Dahlgren chapel erupted into peace.

Over the decades I mentioned this experience a few times, a little more frequently in recent years, but honestly, this is the first time I am writing about it and describing it in some detail.

What took me so long?

I was scared. I now identify with the servant with one talent who buried it in fear of losing it (Matt 25:18). I had no categories to put this experience in, no reasonable thought patterns that fit, no words that expressed that reality, no understanding. I had twelve years of seminary education, multiple week-long retreats, innumerable morning meditations, daily spiritual readings, prayers in varied forms, and a couple of spiritual directors. Nothing prepared me for the light in the Georgetown chapel in 1975.

I didn't talk about it because I didn't know what it was. I didn't think about it because I didn't know how to think about it. I chalked it up to a psychological episode; my emotions were ripe for something unusual, a mid-life reward for being a "good boy." I let it go at that even though I knew that was nonsense—and I wasn't that good of a boy anyway. Back in the safe-deposit box!

Two recent developments coaxed me into looking at the Event more closely. Richard Rohr's invitation to examine the perspectives of the second half of life seems to fit with my Georgetown experience. And our small faith community is exploring mysticism. I am finally, gratefully, and humbly willing to look seriously and honestly at those extraordinary ten minutes. I am no longer afraid.

I now suspect that I was blessed with an intense moment of unmerited Grace. Grace, I am convinced, is not a thing but a relationship with God. Therefore all things and people are graced because we all are in relationship with God. There are "moments of intensity" in this dynamic relationship, and I had an intense one in July 1975 in the Georgetown chapel. I have not had another one like that since. But I guess I don't need another one because I am barely catching up with the first one.

Does anyone need an empty safe-deposit box?

OCTOBER 9, 2015

✧ SIGHTING ✧

The thief left it behind
the moon
at my window!

—RYOKAN

PART TWO

LOVE

God is love. Therefore love. Without distinction, without calculation, without procrastination, love.

—HENRY DRUMMOND

17

Behold the Sun, the Moon, and the Stars

Evander and Fotini Lomke

> *In every human being there is a special*
> *heaven, whole and unbroken.*
>
> —PARACELSUS

The world stopped twenty-three years ago: April 19, 1990.

Our world.

Our bright, curly haired three-and-a-half-year-old Elizabeth closed her eyes and slumped. It was like the sound of a silent crash. For us, an eternity passed in the span of twenty minutes. Little did we know how much life could change over lunch.

It all happened between pediatric appointments, in a hospital cafeteria—no shortage of doctors there. One would eventually tell us that our daughter had a seizure. "She may have epilepsy. She may not. We will give her medication."

What? We hardly knew what epilepsy was. It typically runs in families. Neither of us had any such history.

The medication turned out to be a disaster of side effects and worsening conditions. Others were tried. Combinations. A special unhealthy-sounding regimen called the ketogenic diet involving high-fat consumption. We felt as if we had gone through the looking glass. But if it would help . . .

The seizures became far more intense and frequent. Specialists of every sort were consulted. A degenerative disease was suspected, then ruled out. AIDS was a possibility, though we couldn't imagine how. Tests were often painful. The doctors were looking for diseases too rare and hideous to name.

Finally, a week before Christmas, the chief of pediatric neurology made a diagnosis: Lennox-Gastaut syndrome. LGS is one of the most brutal forms of epilepsy. Even specialists rarely encounter it. We learned there are fifty thousand of these cases. Is that in the United States or the world? Did it matter?

Elizabeth's IQ dropped ninety points: profound retardation as a result of countless petit-mal and grand-mal seizures. By the time she was four she could no longer walk or talk. Since seizures come at night, too, sleep was by fits and starts. How exhausted we three were.

The earth has circled the sun twenty-three times since that April afternoon, as we live day by day with this disabling and ultimately mysterious, overwhelmingly faith-testing syndrome. The more Elizabeth concentrates, for example by being read to, the more seizures she might have. Some seizures have caused her to cry and scream. Others can make her laugh at inappropriate times.

As a twelve-year-old, Elizabeth had a vagus-nerve stimulator (VNS) surgically implanted. She was among the first of her age to receive it, followed by several operations since to change the battery. At the beginning the VNS worked, giving us hope. Fourteen years later the device has a limited positive effect.

Other more experimental treatments and medications have been tried. They only made things worse.

So many times we have asked what Elizabeth had done to deserve this fate? What would become of our little family? Could this be a cross too heavy to be ours?

We have survived these years, and the self-questioning is largely a thing of the past. Yet, after all this time, other, bigger questions remain. How did this soul, with such an extraordinary condition, find two such ordinary people as we? Why us? Why on earth?

Before Elizabeth was born, a dear friend told us that children in heaven choose their parents. We wonder.

We have received all sorts of well-intentioned advice on dealing with the strain. Moving from a school setting, at the age of twenty-one, to day-habilitation meant finding a good program, which is difficult since there are few. As we parents are now in our sixties, there are new, challenging, and painful questions regarding group homes.

The years have taught us a new way to live. Each of us has learned levels of acceptance and ways to grow.

Our faith has been tested. So has our will. They still are. Even more than most, we haven't a clue what tomorrow brings. Life follows a script that the living cannot read.

Being in a medically guarded condition forces us to confront and focus on the plotless, precious present. Elizabeth, and our expectations for her, started out one way. She has blossomed in another.

Although likely for her remaining lifetime to be non-verbal, wheelchair bound, and completely dependent on others for all her needs, she is a beautiful young woman with the spark of life in her eyes and soul.

To us, she is the sun, the moon, and the stars.

We could not imagine life any other way.

JUNE 21, 2013

18

We Talked about Love,
But We Used Hawk Words

Brian Doyle

The last time I saw my brother Kevin in the flesh was three years ago, in his den, in the evening, just before summer began. We sat with our legs sprawled out and talked of hawks and love and pain and Mom and beaches and mathematics and Dad and college and his children and mine and our patient mysterious wives and books and basketball and grace and pain and then hawks again. We were both major serious intent raptor guys, delighted to try to discern the difference between, say, a kestrel and a jay, which are about the same size, although one can dismember a mouse in seconds and the other would faint dead away if dismemberment was on the syllabus.

Both of us would happily have studied hawks for the rest of our lives, but the problem was that his life was ending soon, and this was the last evening we would have to talk about love and hawks, and we knew this, so we talked about hawks and love.

In my experience brothers don't often talk bluntly about love, even if you do love each other inarticulately and thoroughly and confusedly, because it's awkward to talk about love that's not romantic. Everyone chatters and sings and gibbers about romantic love, and how it starts and ends and waxes and wanes, but we hardly ever talk about all the other kinds of love, which include affection and respect and reverence, and also "brothering," which is rough and complicated. Brothers start out in competition and some never stop. Brothers are like trees that start out adjacent but have to grow apart to eat enough light. Brothers worship each other and break each other's noses, and adore each other and steal from each other, and detest each other even as they sprint to defend each other. It's *very* confusing. If you are very lucky you eventually get to be the same age as your brother or brothers. Eventually the differences between and among you erode and dissolve and the love is left in craggy outcrops where you can sit together with your legs sprawled out.

So we talked about love, but we used hawk words. That's what I wanted to tell you this morning. We talked about how it's awfully hard to tell sharp-shinned hawks from Cooper's hawks and who *was* Cooper anyway? We talked about the immeasurably old war between crows and red-tailed hawks, and who started that war, and why, and sure it was about a girl, sure it was. We talked about owls and osprey and eagles and kites and falcons and other raptors too, but mostly we talked about hawks because we knew hawks and saw hawks every day and had always both been addled and thrilled by hawks and we always would be, even after one of us was ashes in a stone box under an oak tree. We talked about how often you can see better with your soul than you can with your eyes in some strange deep true way that I cannot explain even though I have been trying to articulate the inarticulable for a long time. We talked about how one of us promised to stay addled and thrilled by hawks as long as he lived so that both of us would still be delighted by hawks somehow. So it is that now when I see a sharp-shinned hawk sliding sideways through oak branches at supersonic speed in pursuit of a flitter of waxwings, my brother Kevin sees that too, even though the prevailing theory is that he is dead.

Often I find myself mumbling *O my gawd, did you see that?* and he mutters *What could possibly be cooler than that?* and so somehow we are still sprawled and lucky and it is almost summer and we are talking about love.

MAY 20, 2016

19

Marriage Is Two People "In This Thing Together"

Michael Leach

Someone asked the comedian George Burns the secret of a successful marriage. He answered, "That's easy. Marry Gracie."

Marriage is a cosmic crapshoot. You have to be lucky enough to marry the right person, but then you must also be the right person. Marriage is about two people endeavoring to be the right person day in and day out.

Marriage begins when two people vow to go through life as one—to have and to hold in good times and bad—even in death. Actors Ruby Dee and Ossie Davis, married fifty-six years, made their final arrangements early: "Cremation after a public ceremony, and then, into the urn. A special urn, large enough and comfortable enough to hold both of us. Whoever goes first will wait inside for the other. When we are reunited at last, we want the family to say goodbye and seal the urn forever. Then on the side, in letters not too bold—but not too modest either—we want the following inscription: RUBY AND OSSIE—IN THIS THING TOGETHER."

Like marriage itself, that urn with those comingled ashes is an outward sign of inward grace, something sacramental. It represents a promise two people made with all their hearts to participate as one in the life of God for all eternity. Marriage is two souls growing together in love and wisdom and joy, qualities of God that God breathed into their souls at creation.

So married people don't get joy out of marriage, they bring joy to their marriage. If they were killjoys before they got married, they will kill joy in their marriage. Marriage is two people "in this thing together" who work and play and kid around a lot not just because it's enjoyable but because they have seen enough sorrow in the human condition.

Marriage is coming to know someone so well that you both say the same thing at the same time. It's being so close to someone that you think their thoughts and feel their feelings at the same time they think and feel them.

Marriage is being alone together, and being together even when you are alone. It is welcoming others into your circle because it increases your joy.

Marriage is reaching out to the poor, the lonely, and the sick because that is the nature of love just as it is the nature of sunbeams to emanate from the sun. It is teaching your children the same values not by your words but by your life.

Marriage is choosing to have many children or two children or one child or no children at all. It is seeing birth control—the pill, the sponge, the IUD—not as a sin but a blessing.

Young marrieds who want children but can't have them after years of trying will live in full love without children or will adopt them or use artificial insemination. Those who choose the last, like all parents, will watch their children grow like flowers and appreciate them with joy—even though sometimes, when life seems untenable, they, like all people, will wish they had chosen another life.

Marrieds with children suffer every time their toddler scrapes a knee or their child gets bullied or their teenager depressed. They look at their babies and fall in love but worry if they will ever have enough money to put them through college, and they fight about only two things: money and children.

And when they are old they will delight in grandchildren without wanting them to be anything other than what they are, and they will not worry when their adult children pull their hair out. Like the grandmother in the movie *Parenting,* they have come to understand that the roller coaster is more gratifying than the merry-go-round: "Up down, up down. Oh, what a ride! . . . You know, it was just so interesting to me that a ride could make me so frightened, so scared, so sick, so excited, and so thrilled all together! Some didn't like it. They went on the merry-go-round. That just goes around. Nothing. I like the roller coaster. You get more out of it."

Marriage is not only about joy, it is also about mercy. On our twenty-fifth anniversary almost twenty-five years ago Vickie and I sipped champagne at midnight in an empty restaurant on the top floor of the Stamford Hyatt looking at a full moon that spread its one light on rich and poor neighborhoods and shimmered over the waters of Long Island Sound. We confessed to each other that when we met, each of us had tried to manipulate the other into marrying because we knew that the other was someone we could still have fun with fifty years later, be a good parent, a loyal companion, and most of all, our best friend. That was a lovely moment in our marriage. Marriage is two people telling the truth about themselves without fear of being held accountable. They value mercy without strain, an attribute of God that expresses itself as forgiveness without blame.

Marriage is a graduate school for mercy that begins and never seems to end with our self. The miracle is this: when we are the right person but do the wrong thing everything still turns out all right.

Marriage is a loving, long-term companionship that at its heart has little to do with sex or even gender. It is a mutual participation in the love of God. It is a familiarity that breeds content. It is the stuff of life that two people who once were separate and now are one go through. They sometimes hurt each other but want always to help each other. They experience suffering, sorrow, dissatisfaction, and disappointment, but remember the laughter, intimacy, comfort, and joy. They made a promise. They kept it.

First they fell in love. That was the exciting part. Then they learned to love. That was the hard part. Finally, if they were lucky and married the right person and have become the right person, they simply love being loving, and that is the best part.

Marriage is a vocation that reveals the love of God in the lives of two people who are "in this thing together." Unless you've been there, done that, or are learning that, you may not be the best person to tell anyone else what it is.

JULY 28, 2014

20

What Makes a Family?

Jeannine Gramick

What will families from all over the world talk about when they converge in Philadelphia for the World Meeting of Families Congress? I can't help but think about what it *means* to be a family. Is it a marriage license or a wedding ceremony? Is it biological children? Is it both? Or neither?

I think about Kathleen, whose family story captivates me. She grew up in the 1950s in a poor section of Brooklyn with a saintly, hardworking mother, an alcoholic father who beat his wife, two brothers (the younger of whom she helped raise), and an older sister who often scolded her.

"The toughest struggle we faced was not poverty but a combination of sexism, alcoholism, and domestic violence," Kathleen told me. She found consolation and peace in daily mass and novenas, even though no one in her family was a churchgoer. Kathleen felt happy and safe during that hour, and her faith in a kind and loving Father-God grew.

At age sixteen she met a man three years older who showered her with attention. They married two years later, at a time when life decisions were made upon high school graduation. Three children were born within thirteen years. Kathleen loved being a mother, but her husband wanted her entire attention and resented the time she spent with their children. Their relationship grew strained, and they became increasingly quarrelsome with each other.

"I turned to my faith and prayed for guidance," Kathleen said. Eventually she met a young woman named Honour who would become a close friend, support, and confidante during this trying time.

On a Cursillo weekend at church, Kathleen spoke with a priest about her home life. Expecting to be told that she needed to try harder to make the marriage work, she was surprised when the priest assured her that she should not feel guilty, that she was a good wife and mother, and that her husband needed to change. When she shared this advice with her husband, he too was surprised. Although he never attended church, he expected the priest to counsel Kathleen to obey her husband. Shortly thereafter, there was another shock.

"When my husband didn't come home one day, I asked my neighbor if she had seen him," Kathleen told me. "Yes, he left this morning with suitcases in hand," her neighbor told her. He never came back, but he let Kathleen know that he did not want custody of the children, only the car and a way to pay his debts. They got a divorce.

For years Kathleen worked hard to support her children and pay off all the loans. Throughout this time Honour was her lifeblood. Kathleen looked forward to each evening, when they would meet to share what happened during the day. She felt joy whenever Honour was around and missed her when they were apart. After some time they both came to realize that their companionship had blossomed into something deeper.

"Our wonderful friendship evolved into the beautiful love we've now shared for over thirty years," Kathleen told me. Although neither Kathleen nor Honour had ever been in a lesbian relationship, they wanted to be committed to each other in a unique way.

They naturally wanted to live together, but given the "talk" that Kathleen's children would endure in the intolerant atmosphere of the 1980s, they decided to wait until the youngest daughter departed for Fordham University. Finally, they claimed a home of their own, but not an exclusive one; their home was always open to others in need.

For example, when Kathleen's granddaughter was sexually abused, the seventeen-year-old found protection and comfort with Kathleen and Honour for more than two years while she finished college and started on a career. Kathleen's eyes lit up as she remembered those days: "We did everything together as a family. We would discuss current events and what she learned at school. Honour and I just loved having her youthful energy around us!"

When Kathleen's mother needed care, she lived her last ten years with Kathleen and Honour. "We had dinner with my mother, played many games of Scrabble in the evenings, took her to mass on Sunday and to practically everywhere we went," Kathleen said. When the diocese approved a support group for families of LGBT Catholics, they brought her to the gatherings. "She really enjoyed getting together with other parents at the church," Kathleen recalled.

Both Kathleen and Honour had profound spiritual longings and attended mass together. "I've always had a deep, visceral connection with my Catholic faith," Kathleen said. "I'm not sure that the church will ever change its views about lesbian and gay people, but I firmly believe my relationship with Honour is a blessing God bestowed on me. All the opposition we encountered from society and church teachings could never shatter my trust that our love is a gift from God, and I am so grateful for this gift."

I've meditated a lot on Kathleen's amazing story and about the meaning of a family. I think about her family when she was a child growing up. Society and church would say that they were a family because they were a mother, a father, and four biological children. Sure, they may have been a highly dysfunctional family, where physical beatings and the fear of drunken rages were simply normal fare. But still, they were a family, weren't they?

I think about her family life with her husband. Yes, they had a marriage license for one man and one woman for more than twenty years. Kathleen with her husband and children must be a family, even though his suspicion, jealousy, and total lack of interest in the children or in supporting them were demolishing the spousal relationship. Yes, they must be a family, even though her husband would not seek counseling or therapy because, as he said, he did not need to change.

I think about her life with Honour and their time with Kathleen's mother and granddaughter. For most of their years together, Kathleen and Honour had no marriage license and they had no biological children from their union. What they did have was the deepest kind of love I have encountered—the love of sacrifice for each other, for those they care about, and for those in need, the love of putting the other's happiness and welfare first, the love of never speaking a cross word to each other, the love of common spiritual values, the love of feeling uniquely blessed by God because of the other.

The love of Kathleen and Honour makes me think of the theme of the World Meeting of Families Congress: "Love Is Our Mission: The Family Fully Alive."

JULY 17, 2015

21

For a Short Time
We Were Jackson's Family

Mark Redmond

I work with homeless, runaway, and at-risk teenagers at Spectrum Youth and Family Services in Burlington, Vermont. Several years ago a nineteen-year-old man named Jackson showed up at our drop-in center for a hot meal, and when we found out he was living in a car, we invited him into our shelter. Spectrum's mission is to serve as family for those youth who, for whatever reason, have none at that moment. And in my mind, a family does not let one of its own live in a car.

A few months later one of our board members hosted a house party that some of our staff attended, and one of them brought Jackson along to say a few words to those present. I listened to him speak about his life and about how grateful he was for the help he was receiving from us. I've worked with thousands of homeless young people over the last four decades, and in my mind Jackson stood out because of the kindness and sincerity that radiated from him.

He always had a job while with us, but what Jackson wanted more than anything else was to join the Marines. I didn't encourage him, nor did I discourage him. The military can be a good character-building experience for some people who have had a difficult life up until that point, but it can also be overwhelming for others.

Jackson applied, was accepted, and shipped out to boot camp in Parris Island, South Carolina.

Jackson wrote me, and it sounded like he was doing fine. When it was time for him to graduate from boot camp, I knew that none of his birth family would be there, so I asked one of our staff members to fly down and be with him at the ceremony.

Jackson phoned me the day of his graduation. He sounded thrilled. "We are so proud of you," I told him. "Congratulations!"

Things spiraled downward. Jackson transitioned on to the next phase of military training, and to this day I don't know what happened, but within a few weeks he was in trouble and then discharged. I called and called to get some sense of what was going on, but I couldn't reach him and had no luck getting any information from the Marines.

Soon the staff in our drop-in center let me know that Jackson was back in Burlington and occasionally coming around for a meal. I told them: "Please have him contact me as soon as you see him again. Tell him he can come back and live with us if he wants to." But I didn't hear from him.

A month later I was on my computer at home on a Saturday night and pulled up the online version of the *Burlington Free Press* to see what was going on that day. I saw a headline about a suicide. A young man had led police on a high-speed chase and then killed himself with a gun.

It was Jackson.

A few days later a wake was held for him at a funeral home in the town where he had grown up. I went to it with several others from Spectrum. Our hearts ached.

There was an obituary in the paper, with the standard line to the effect of, "He leaves behind the loving family of . . . " But a few days later a woman phoned me who identified herself as having been a neighbor to Jackson and his family when he was growing up.

"That obituary was a lie," she said. "There was no loving family for Jackson. If he had a loving family at all, it was you people at Spectrum."

She told me that her son and Jackson had been close childhood friends, but for some reason the friendship ended. She didn't know why, but right before he entered the Marines, Jackson came to see her son, all these years later. He told her son that when they were little he had once stolen some Pokémon cards from him, and he now wanted to apologize.

She told me it spoke volumes about the kind of person Jackson was. I agreed.

When you come into our office at Spectrum today there are several group photos of young people on the wall by the entrance. Jackson is in one of them, having dinner with a bunch of the other kids in the house, a big smile on his face. The staff member we flew down to Parris Island is gone, and only one other person besides me who works at Spectrum even remembers Jackson now. Everyone else employed here walks by that photo every day, not knowing the story behind that one young man's smile.

But I know who he is. He was a tender soul who, like many of the kids with whom we work, had endured great suffering early on in life. For some people that kind of suffering results in a personality filled with bitterness. Jackson always revealed gratitude.

The definition of family means different things to different people. And as that woman who called me stated, we at Spectrum were Jackson's family, at least for a brief period. We are there for young people when they need us, in whatever way they need us. That's what a family is, that's what a family does. Jackson may not have had much happiness in his life, but at least for a short while he was surrounded by people who cared about him and loved him. I believe he knew that, and my soul finds comfort in his knowing.

JANUARY 26, 2018

22

Mercy Is a Child Named Jaden

Barbara Danko Garland

When the time arrived for Elizabeth to have her child she gave birth to a son. Her neighbors and relatives heard that the Lord had shown his great mercy toward her, and they rejoiced with her.

*—*LUKE 1:57–58

I sang at their wedding. My husband, Brian, played the piano. I sat in the choir week after week and watched them loving each other. I was happy for them. Then her belly began to grow and a pain that is indescribable infected every part of my being.

"Dear God, I beg you. Please let me be at peace. All those stories about women getting pregnant in the Bible, can't I be one? I beg you. Let me truly be happy and not envious as her belly grows . . . as her baby is born, cries, nurses, is baptized, and clings to her . . . *please.*"

I cried.

How could I have such a deep desire to have a child and face the reality of infertility?

So Brian and I began the journey of seeking a child through adoption. Resentment for the process crept in like a rat in the corner of my consciousness; as introverted as I am, why did I have to divulge so much information about my life to strangers and then wait for them to approve me as a parent?

"O my God, help me. Help me. Help me. Help me! Where are you? I beg you. Please just take the desire to have children away. Please, give me peace!"

Dear Mr. and Mrs. Garland,

Due to the fact that no one is coming to us seeking parents for their children, you will have to find a child on your own.

Sincerely,

Your local Catholic adoption agency

More resentment. Disappointment. Grief.

Then a miracle happened.

An act of mercy revealed as an idea.

God was answering my prayers with a direction that was always in front of us but that we never discerned. Brian and I knew, just knew, with an absolute peace in our hearts that only God can give, that we should foster to adopt.

"His name is Jaden. He's five. Do you want to meet him? Be careful not to fall in love too quickly. Take it slowly."

We met him in a parking lot of a local farmer's market, halfway between his current foster parents and us. It was biting cold. He had no gloves or hat and wore a hoodie. He held on for a moment to the foster mother with whom he had so quickly been placed when his former foster father of three years was in a serious accident. She was doing the best she could.

"Jaden, these friends of mine are going to watch you for a while today."

I had never met her in my life. She was my friend. I hugged her.

After a minute of shyness, Jaden talked nonstop for the forty-minute car ride about his foster families, his favorite color, green (which quickly became blue when he learned that was our favorite color), his biological brothers, his favorite TV show, *Little Einsteins*, and anything else that sprung into his mind. He expressed pleasure that that we were going to McDonalds, his favorite fast-food restaurant. But even in all that talking he asked us for nothing. He trusted us with everything—this little being who didn't even know he should wonder who these people were.

When we got out of the car, I squatted down in front of him to be at his level to talk and found myself gazing into big grayish-blue eyes that, like mine, wanted only the assurance of peace.

"What do you want to eat?" I asked him.

It happened so quickly, he startled me. He reached up with his little five-year-old hands, touched my hair, leaned over, and kissed my cheek. I was flooded with a love I had never known, a love that healed my envy, dissolved resentment, answered every question. My heart was his.

Two weeks later Jaden moved in with us.

Four weeks later I cradled him in my arms, his body tucked close to mine, and he asked: "Barbara, can I call you Mommy, and Brian, Daddy?"

"Yes, Jaden, you can."

"And you can call me Baby."

"The Lord had shown great mercy to her."

Yes, in that sweet, tiny voice, God showed mercy and, like Elizabeth, I rejoiced.

It's been two years now, and God continues to shower us with mercy through Jaden: in his crying because he felt so special at his baptism; in wanting to sing in the choir with us on Sunday mornings; in his excitement to put up the song numbers at church; in playing with a classmate at school who is shy; in his evening prayers every night "for everyone in the world and for everyone in heaven"; in the thrill he showed after his first reconciliation; in his peaceful grayish-blue eyes as we tuck him into bed each night.

God's time is not our time. In all of these things, and countless others, I thank God for the mercy that is birthing every moment, whether we know it at the time or not.

APRIL 8, 2016

23

A Good Man
Is Not Hard to Find

Michael Leach

You are my sunshine, my only sunshine.
You make me happy when skies are gray.
You'll never know dear, how much I love
    you.
Please don't take my sunshine away.

Gene Conrad, eighty-six years old, got up every morning at 5 to make breakfast for his wife, Reva. Before he shuffled downstairs he cuddled next to her and began singing the song they had sung to each other every morning since they married in 1950: "You Are My Sunshine." Reva was diagnosed with Alzheimer's twenty-one years ago, but she glowed as she heard the words Gene sang. Gene died last week after a brief illness. . . .

I'm sitting in a circle with nine other guys in a meeting room at Union Memorial Church in Stamford,

Connecticut, remembering Gene Conrad. We are members of a support group he began and moderated for men whose wives have dementia, one of only a handful in the country. Union was Gene's parish. He was a deacon and trustee.

We're joined this afternoon by the pastor, Rev. Blaine Edele, a trim fellow much younger than the rest of us. "Their daughters placed Reva in Waverly House when Gene died," he informs us, "the best facility around. Gene had it all set up. He had everything set up long before he died. The girls didn't tell Reva that Gene had passed. That would have been unkind. She would forget it in a minute anyway. She's adjusting well."

Pastor Blaine shares memories of Gene. "When Reva was diagnosed, he challenged himself to find out as much about the disease as he could, to learn how to be the best caregiver to her he could be. He was a researcher by profession, you know, a PhD in medical science. When I asked him what advice I should give to caregivers, he said without a beat: 'Caregiving is noble, rewarding but frustrating. Patience is both a virtue and a necessity.'"

The guys in the room nod and share knowing glances. Blaine continues. "Gene never felt he or Reva was a victim. He saw the experience as an opportunity to become wiser, more nurturing, more tender, more mature. As he explained it to me, as much as it is a relief for a caregiver to provide comfort for his spouse, the enduring reward is the wisdom that comes from learning what life is really all about."

Blaine then passes the spiritual baton to Paul, the logical successor to Gene as group moderator. Paul has the craggy good looks of a retired TV anchor. Gravitas is in his bones. As he remembers Gene, I remember Paul's story. His wife, Joan, has been in a near vegetative state for five years. He visits her in the nursing home every day. He once shared: "When I come into her room and sit at her side, I ask her, 'Where is my kiss?' and, amazingly, she puckers up. Her eyes are closed. She can't talk. The only real communication is when I feed her. Her mouth opens up just like a little bird." Paul hangs around the home and visits patients who don't get visitors and makes a fuss over them.

"Your turn, Mike," Paul says. "Is there anything particular you remember?"

"I remember Reva was here once," I recall, "and she was sitting over there and I went over to her and sat down and held her hand and talked to her. Her skin was translucent, like it was made of light, like many old people, and she had a kind face. I told her Gene was a good man. She nodded vigorously and her whole face broke into this crazy happy smile. Here she was, long past the expiration date for Alzheimer's, and still young and charming. I remembered Gene telling us how they sang 'You are my sunshine' every morning and I could see them and hear them, and you gotta believe that sunshine will follow them forever."

It's Peter's turn. He's the youngest of us, in his early sixties. Kathy, his wife of forty years, died last year after suffering twenty years through seven forms of cancer and early onset Alzheimer's for four. Peter once said, "I know how difficult it is for a husband whose wife has forgotten his name, but I'd give anything just to be back at that place again." Peter is a deacon in his church. He will soon move to Weston, Massachusetts, where he will study to become a priest at Pope St. John XXIII National Seminary. "It's a vocation I think I've felt for fifty years," he says. "Now I am ready for it." Peter was with Gene in the hospital the day he died. "I heard him say one thing, 'I'm ready.'"

Paul asks Len if he'd like to share anything. Len tries to speak but chokes up. Tears squeeze out of the corners of his eyes. "I can't," he says. "Later." Len is a powerful man who looks like he was a fullback in high school. He needs to be strong because his wife, Sabina, can't talk or walk and there is a lot of heavy lifting to get her out of bed, onto the toilet, into the shower, onto the stair lift, into a wheelchair, into the car, over and over again. "This is my purpose," he once shared with us. "It's my life. This is what I'm here for. It's what I do. I can't imagine life without her."

The invisible baton moves around the circle, Art, Bob, Dick, Henri, all the way to Stan, the oldest of us at ninety-five. And just like that our hour is up.

"Len?" says Paul. "Would you like the last word?"

Len again has trouble getting out the words. He shakes his head and says, "Gene meant so much to us. He was a good listener."

We will meet again in two weeks. Pastor Blaine tells us the room is ours for as long as we want. We leave the church in twos and threes, into the sunshine.

SEPTEMBER 25, 2015

✧ SIGHTING ✧

Early one morning on the steps of Precious Blood Church, a woman with cancer on the face was begging (beggars are allowed only in the slums) and when I gave her money (no sacrifice on my part but merely passing on alms which had been given me) she tried to kiss my hand. The only thing I could do was kiss her dirty old face with the gaping hole in it where an eye and a nose had been. It sounds like a heroic deed but it was not. One gets used to ugliness so quickly. What we avert our eyes from one day is easily borne the next when we have learned a little more about love. Nurses know that, and so do mothers.

—DOROTHY DAY, THE LONG LONELINESS

24

Construct No Walls around Sacred Space

Francine Dempsey

Images of endless war, overflowing refugee camps, hate-filled terrorists, billion-dollar weapons, starved children—I want to flee this world's violence. So I ask my prayer group, women who, like me, have lived through many decades totally safe from such horrible experiences, "What am I to do?"

Eighty-five-year-old Pat says, "I'm reading *The Letters of Etty Hillesum*." I recall from a long-ago reading of her diaries and letters, *An Interrupted Life,* that Etty died in a concentration camp during the Holocaust.

Joanne explains that while imprisoned by German invaders in Westerbork, a concentration camp near her Netherlands home, Etty wrote numerous letters to family and friends. While each day she watched as guards packed a train's boxcars with human cargo bound for Auschwitz and death—simply for being Jews—she wrote letters filled with stories of men and women doing good.

I find a library copy of Etty's book.

Throughout her letters Etty describes the human suffering but also the human goodness that happens day after day, week after week, month after month, as the trains come, again and again. I ponder Etty's words: "Despite everything, life is full of beauty and meaning." And, "We have been marked by suffering for a whole lifetime. And yet life in its unfathomable depths is so wonderfully good."

One day it is Etty's turn to board her boxcar in the train that also carries her parents to Auschwitz. In her final written words, discovered on a postcard she throws from the moving train, Etty, a woman of deep spirituality, quotes her Bible: "The Lord is my high tower." Of herself and her mother and father, weakened and ill after their Westerbork life of near starvation, exposure to extreme heat, cold, overcrowded rooms, and mattress-less bunks, Etty proclaims: "We left the camp singing."

I ask myself, can Westerbork, a place of unimaginable human suffering, be a sacred place or holy ground, maybe even more so than the pure, placid, peaceful church or synagogue or mosque or temple space?

Can I image Syria, or Afghanistan, or Yemen, or Sudan, or Somalia, or a refugee camp holding 180,000, places of war and famine, death and starvation, as places where human goodness endures, as sacred places "full of meaning and beauty," where angels and humans are singing a chorus of beauty in the midst of ugliness?

This is a struggle in two ways. First, I know belief in human goodness everywhere must not blind me to the horrors of violent war, of raging famine. I must not be a Pollyanna, must never stop my efforts to end endless war, to assist refugees and victims of famine, to resist injustice, including my own, in its many forms. Yet I must at the same time know that I am walking in a sacred space with truly holy men and women in war zones and refugee camps, doing endless acts of human kindness, of love, amid their suffering, even their suffering unto death.

Second, like Etty, I must face my willingness to construct walls around my comforting image of sacred space, my letting into the sacred space only the imprisoned, the suffering, while excluding the "other," the perpetrators of the violence—the enemy. Etty struggles with God's command to love all in a much more difficult situation. But she refuses to let hate into her heart. Of the guards she says, "I have never been so frightened of anything in my life. I sank to my knees with the words that preside over human life; And God made man after His likeness. That passage spent a difficult morning with me."

So in my born-a-Catholic heart I must struggle with "love your enemies," "they know not what they do," "I have come to save sinners." In God, there is only one sacred space.

Like most twenty-first-century religious pushing eighty, I am called by the new creation story, new science, new theology. I am learning of the "oneness" that in recent years scientists and theologians pose as the heart of reality.

Since 2000 my community has called me to prayer that seeks oneness, communion: centering prayer, contemplative prayer, even mystical prayer. In this world so fractured, so full of noise, religious community members, like so many others, are seeking to find that deep silence, deep prayer, deep connection with God, so essential to knowing our oneness with God and all that is in God, and bringing that oneness to all.

So with Etty's help I reconstruct my image of sacred space. Can I in my heart hold *all* as sacred? Each night in my prayer I wrap God's encircling, unconditional love around the suffering and the inflictors of the suffering, and yes, they are one with me.

SEPTEMBER 8, 2017

25

Soulful Connections Spring from a Prison Writing Program

Marybeth Christie Redmond

The last thing on earth I anticipated as a vocation was writing with addicted, mentally ill inmates inside a prison facility. These women, ages twenty to sixty-five, at Chittenden Correctional Facility in Northern Vermont, have dealt drugs, driven drunk, abused children, embezzled employers, robbed convenience stores at gunpoint, and even murdered their own kin. They have also taught me to become a more vulnerable person and about reservoirs of mercy and compassion I never knew I had.

I came to this work as a journalist covering marginalized communities for twenty-five years. More advocate than reporter, I always battled a desire to change systems rather than cover them objectively, a bit of a deal breaker for a journalist.

But despite past encounters with jailed persons and correctional systems, I was unprepared for the profound and soulful connections I would develop with Vermont's incarcerated women by writing weekly with them for four years. Nor could I anticipate the life lessons they would bequeath me.

Most prison volunteers don't want to know the gory details of inmate transgressions, but to be honest, I'm interested. I want to challenge myself to the depths of living an authentic Christ-centered life. Can I encounter what society sees as the most broken, vile ones—the bottom of the human "food chain"—and behold the face of Christ, feel the energy of Christ? Can I surmount the human recoil factor in myself and receive these voiceless ones as Jesus did?

I could certainly roam the hallways of Chittenden emanating Pollyanna-like mercy to counteract the chaos of clanging metal doors, officers barking commands, an environment void of color, and women in severe stress. Yet a greater challenge would be to enter this highly prescribed world open and be receptive, as Jesus did in the life-changing encounters of his day. I am learning that transformation comes not from trying to change other people, but from the vulnerability needed to shift the way we see and experience them.

As a result, when co-founder Sarah Bartlett and I began the Writing Inside VT program in 2010 within the state's singular women's prison, we made a decision to write as vulnerable participants. The purpose of the program is to use writing as a tool for self-change and to build healthy community. So we too put pen to page to see with a fresh eye our own struggles with depression, dysfunctional relationships, underemployment, and varied experiences of marginalization. It seemed critical that a sacred space be created "inside" where mutual relationships could exist and Holy Spirit–level transformation could swoop in unannounced for each of us alike.

And that is precisely what has resulted. Our ever-changing circle of fifteen to eighteen weekly writers has congealed into a tightknit community of women who learn, practice, grieve, hope, vision, and celebrate together, where there is nothing to whitewash in past or present lives. More than two hundred imprisoned women have participated in Writing Inside VT, writing toward self-change and building a community of trust.

On a given night, through her prose, Stacy shows us what unbridled anger looks like when you've grown up in a household that fails to provide for your safety and security. We all learn to be less afraid of rage:

I'm bleeding, but no one cares. I am alone. A goldfish among sharks. A sheep in wolf's clothing. I try to blend in, but my heart gives me away. I am scared, confused, forced to be someone I'm not. Made to believe it was the only way.

Raven models for us a deep acceptance of self and the quirks that uniquely mark each one of us as part of the human condition:

They say, "crazy, nuts, cuckoo," yet they whisper, "shh, she's mentally ill."

They say, "off her rocker, in la-la land," yet they whisper, "shh, she's mentally ill."

I begin to whisper, "smart, confident, a good person and mom," yet I think, "I am mentally ill."

Why am I mentally ill? Why are we whispering?

I go to my safe place where I crouch and can hardly breathe.

I whisper, "I am not mentally ill, I am just merely me."

Through the poetry of Tess, we learn what authentic surrender to the Divine sounds like when battling an insidious addiction (as we all do, in some form or another):

> It is me your daughter.
> I am here in your light,
> broken before you.
> Please show me what it is
> you want from me.
> I am at your mercy;
> I am on bended knee,
> asking for you to hold me,
> comfort me, show me how
> to control my fear of the world.

It is a favorite prayer I keep tucked within the nightstand to murmur to the good Lord in my own anxiety-wracked hours.

And then there's Norajean, who calls herself a "slightly cracked child of God." Reincarcerated again, she pours herself into the writing each time. Her words help us understand how deep wounds can reach inside:

> Those of us who survive here
> by reading scars
> finding faults
> before they open up and swallow us
> talk gingerly.
> We learned early
> to whisper, tiptoe, skirt
> our way around.
> We, who live by losing
> love and letting go,
> endure random uprooting.

The writers' penetrating honesty provides a springboard from which to unpack my own past difficulties. As I give voice to unclaimed aspects of my life, I feel inner strength regenerating, and the "inside" women who hear my stories feel less alone:

> Piles of psychic wreckage
> sometimes border
> on landfill scale.
> I step along the surface,
> picking and sorting
> through the heap
> of composting emotions.

When a person has been brought to her proverbial knees, there is nothing left to protect. I walk freely in a world beyond prison walls but have learned much from these incarcerated women's humble stance. Their lives challenge us all to coexist vulnerably with each another, to free up guarded places, fulfill unrealized visions, and speak our own truths to power.

And just as these women recover self-worth by learning to see themselves and others with the eye of their soul, so too must society at large receive the voices of its most marginalized members in order to evolve. At first this humble stance fits us as uneasily as an orange jump suit or the like, but it will empower us "to put on the clothes of Jesus Christ" (Rom 13:14) and see and be with "the least of these my brothers and sisters" (Matt 25:40) in the core of our being.

DECEMBER 6 2013

26

Homeless Mother Lets the Cruel Knife Drop

Jade Angelica

Homeless people were part of my daily life when I lived in Cambridge, Massachusetts. They begged for money at the corner by the 7-Eleven. They held signs asking for work at the traffic light coming off the Mass Pike. They gathered for warmth on the grates over the subway tunnel around the corner from Harvard Square. One woman slept each night at the doorway to Bank of America.

Now, living in a small town in Iowa where the homeless population is as invisible as unwanted mice, I was shocked when someone told me that children in Dubuque were sleeping in cars. "How many children?" I wanted to know. HomeAid America, a national nonprofit that provides housing for the homeless, estimates that 3.5 million Americans are homeless each year, including one million children on any given night. The Dubuque School District serves more than two hundred homeless children.

That seemed impossible to me. But then I met Jen. She and her four children, ages four to fifteen, were living at

Maria House, a shelter opened in 2000 through the efforts of six Catholic women's religious communities. There are many reasons given for homelessness, including child abuse, domestic violence, PTSD from military service, and natural disasters. Jen explained to me how it happened to her.

Jen grew up in a middle-class family in Dubuque. After graduating from high school, she married young, had children, and did not pursue further education. Over the years her husband's physical abuse escalated, and finally Jen fled, with only her children and the clothes they were wearing. She fled to her mother's home, where they lived peacefully for a while. Then the internal and external pressure to be a part of a couple (the *need* to have a man in her life, as Jen described it) became overpowering. She met a man who seemed charming and attentive, and she moved in with him.

This charmer, a meth addict and dealer, introduced Jen to meth, and she quickly became addicted. Soon they both were arrested. He was convicted of manufacturing meth in their home; she was convicted of endangering her children. Jen's children were placed in foster care.

After being released from prison, Jen, now a felon, was not eligible for government-subsidized housing. So her mother paid for her to live in a weekly hotel, and Jen got her children back. But she didn't—she couldn't—stop using drugs. Eventually her mother ran out of money and couldn't afford the hotel. Wisely, no one Jen knew would take in a drug-addicted mom and four children, so she moved her family into a tent at Dubuque's riverside Miller

Park. They lived there for months, even when rain and hail battered their tent. Jen was high most of that time, trying to numb herself to the reality of her life. But then, on a cold September night, during a moment of sobriety (she had run out of money for buying drugs), she took a good look at her two youngest children. They were shivering and crying from the cold. For a split second Jen connected with them. She recognized their suffering and was overcome by compassion for her children. She began to weep.

"I hated myself," she told me. "I loved my children." This one, rare, sober moment of connection, clarity, and compassion changed Jen's life. She called her mother that night and said she was ready for the hard work of rehab. Two days later Jen was admitted to inpatient rehab in Des Moines, her children safely placed with family.

Two years later Jen is still clean and sober. She works full time as a restaurant manager, and for the first time is self-supporting and living independently. With guidance from the Maria House staff, Jen learned the skills needed to become a capable worker and a responsible single parent. A humble, recovering addict, she freely shares her story to inspire others. "I no longer beat myself up," she told me. "I am learning how to care for myself and my kids."

Jen's not religious, so she doesn't tell her story with "there by the grace of God" language. As a spiritual director, however, I endeavor to see Jen's story with eyes of the soul and recognize the presence of grace at work in our lives. As I struggled to write these words about what

I saw happening for Jen, the words of the Sufi poet Hafiz enlightened me about the impact of encounters with God:

> Once a young woman said to me, "Hafiz,
> what is the sign of someone who
>   knows God?"
> I became very quiet, and looked
> deep into her eyes, then replied,
> "My dear, they have dropped the knife.
>   Someone
> who knows God has dropped the cruel
>   knife
> that most so often use upon their ten-
>   der self
> and others."

For Jen, that moment of vision was a communion with God—whether she knew to name it that or not—and it became her turning point. She dropped the cruel knife that had been visited upon her and that she used on herself and her children. And it remains dropped.

We all have luminous moments, as Jen did at the homeless campsite. Our first challenge is to see them. Our second challenge is to say yes. Only then can the knife fall and healing begin.

NOVEMBER 4, 2016

27

When the Soul Sees Desperate Need, It Does Not Turn Away

Gerald Kicanas

They are coming from Syria, Iraq, Afghanistan, and count-less other places that are difficult or dangerous to live in. They are mostly young men, but there are many families as well. They have left behind everything: their jobs, their homes, their belongings, their security. They left desper-ate to get away from violence, war, the death of family and friends, the impossibility of finding work to sustain themselves. They left wanting to find a safer place for their children to live and to grow up with some semblance of dignity.

They travel several routes to get to the West. Each route is challenging and risks the loss of their lives.

In Belgrade, Serbia, I met two young Afghan boys, twelve and thirteen years of age, following the Balkan Route, with the dream of going to London where one boy has a relative. They were crossing into Serbia from Bulgaria, a place that so many migrants say is difficult and dangerous. They were treated poorly. The police hit them. Thugs stole their money and cell phones. The boys were in a vehicle with twenty people jammed together and jolting into each like dice being shaken by an angry hand. The driver, a smuggler, was drunk and speeding. Suddenly the truck turned over. One boy broke his arm. The other sprained his neck. But they were alive. Not all lived.

The boys expressed gratefulness for the support they are receiving in Serbia from Catholic Relief Services (CRS) and Caritas Serbia. "People care," they told me. "You feel respected." Now they hope to get into Hungary, whose borders are closed, and eventually into Western Europe. They heard of mistreatment in Hungary and heard the country wants no part of them. Yet they want to go forward following their dream.

These boys, along with nearly three hundred mostly Afghans, were living in barracks CRS is refurbishing into space that gives some privacy and dignity to the refugees. There they feel safe and have their needs met.

In Athens I encountered two men in a CRS, Caritas Hellas Center who followed the Mediterranean Route. Ahmed was from Syria and Assam from Afghanistan. Ahmed has five children including a fifteen-day-old child, and Assam two children. Ahmed was a chef and owned a restaurant in Syria. Assam had very little schooling and did odd jobs.

Ahmed left because of the war in Syria. He teared up talking about friends who were killed. He wanted to get his family out. He was terrified, crowded in a small dingy boat sailing from Turkey to Greece in stormy conditions. "We had to throw our belongings overboard so the boat would not sink. I prayed that if any of my family died, we would all die so we would not be separated." They paid smugglers fifteen hundred euros to cross from Syria to Turkey and one thousand euros per person to cross from Turkey to Greece.

Assam spoke of living in fear in his country and desiring only to get his children out of there so they could live a decent life and get an education, which he never got. His only dream was that they have a future. He would do anything to assure that.

Both men said that if those who fear and reject refugees lived in the conditions in which they lived they would do what they did, get out as quickly as possible regardless of the risk. No one can stand their children being in jeopardy.

They expressed countless times their appreciation to CRS and Caritas Hellas for saving them, for giving them dignity, for restoring their pride and self-confidence.

CRS is leasing empty apartment buildings in Athens for families awaiting resettlement. There are so many empty buildings after the economic disaster of 2010 that CRS can find reasonable rents to help people get out of camps, where they live in tents, and into some respectable housing.

At the dock in Piraeus, just outside of Athens, you see tent after tent on both sides of the road housing mostly Syrian and Afghan families and young men. There are few services provided, but many Greek people, in spite of their own economic difficulties, are helping provide food, medicine, clothing, and other needs of the refugees.

You have to admire the Serbian and Greek people who understand they are their brother's keeper. When you see desperate need with the eye of your soul you don't turn away, walk away, but you stop as did the Good Samaritan and you do what you can. Many are doing what they can even though their own conditions are desperate.

One family living in a tent in Piraeus asked Carolyn Woo, president of CRS, "Why have you come? Was it only to take pictures, to feel good, or was it to help?" Haunting question! Why was I here? Just to look, to observe, or to act? I remembered the words from St. James's letter, "Suppose a brother or a sister is without clothes and daily food. If one of you says to them, 'Go in peace; keep warm and well fed,' but does nothing about their physical needs, what good is it?"

All around us there is a needy world on the move, brothers and sisters desperately seeking a better way of life. I need to do what little I can to alleviate some of that suffering. We all do.

AUGUST 12, 2016

28

The Street Girls of India Were Just Little Girls After All

Paul Wilkes

They stopped at the doorway.

It was dark within, damp, with chunks of concrete on the floor. They had been in such places before, many times. They knew to be wary. What danger might lurk inside if they dared to go further?

But today it was different. I felt a tiny hand in my right hand, then my left. Tentatively, we moved forward, their tiny flip-flops crunching across the rough floor, echoing from the bare walls.

Slowly, so very slowly, a small but brightening smile washed over their faces.

These were my children—adopted, in a way—the street girls of India. They had slept in buildings under construction before—there are so many in booming India—stealthily sneaking in as workers left, quickly leaving before they arrived the next morning. But this was not to be a temporary, furtive shelter. It would soon be their home in Secunderabad, India.

They led me to the light, a window opening, to see what they would view each morning when they awoke. They ran their free hand over the thin shelf of poured concrete—this would be their cubby, holding their few possessions. Ah, but it would have a lock. And they, and they alone, would hold the key.

Strange, that I was standing here with them, no longer a reporter telling a story, but rather a partner with them in their quest for a safe refuge from the angry and dangerous streets of India.

It began, as most wonderful things in our lives, by sheer chance. Or perhaps because of that Mischievous One who, every so often, whispers softly and tantalizingly, "Something interesting going on. . . . Hold on for a minute. . . . Slow down friend. . . . Take a look." (What reporter can resist that?)

I was a tourist in India in 2006, brought by accident to an orphanage run by Salesian sisters. A little girl stood before me, her eye a swirl of dead tissue. Blinded. To make her a "better" beggar. My wince. Her smile. One chapter of my life was coming to an end, another was opening.

The desire was unfocused, a strategic plan lacking, but I wanted to do something for her and her friends, the or-phaned, neglected, and abandoned ones. Ten dollars here, a hundred there . . . somehow the donations came in. I started a nonprofit, calling it Home of Hope, the English version of Prathyasha Bhavan, the Hindi name for her shelter. And today Secunderabad is one of four orphanages we have built in India. Five hundred girls—a half dozen of them with me right now—would not be raped or beaten or murdered. They would not be chattel in the sex trade. They would be safe with the sisters, eat healthily, go to school. They would have the opportunity for a productive, dignified life.

For the next few months my girls would still be sleeping, jammed in, as they have been for too many years, head to head, in rows on another concrete floor, this in an upper room of a tiny house. Sixty-five of them. But soon this would be their home. They would have a bed, a luxury few of them had ever experienced.

Further into the room they walked, now more confident, letting go of my hand. They were in *their* place now. Their eyes moved from unfinished wall to unfinished wall, as if standing in a palace. So grand, so large; somehow they were already seeing it, filled with the bunk beds they had only seen in pictures, a bright bedspread that they would be able to choose. A pillow, a soft pillow on which to lay their head.

They stood atop the mounds of cement and sand that would soon be leveled into a fine, smooth floor that they would keep clean, oh, so clean. They were just little girls after all—who could resist such a vantage point, such a feeling of majesty? For once they could look down, not be looked down upon.

The years before, my life before, had been filled with its own moments. Standing to applause at receiving an award, seeing my byline in *The New Yorker*, on the spine of a book, many books.

But there was none of that at this moment, just two little hands finding mine once more as we headed for the doorway. A gaze back, as if to make sure it was real. Then, looking up at me, another kind of smile, at once so simple and shy, yet so radiant, a message from the heart and soul of girls who were about to have their first real home.

March 14, 2014

29

What I Learned about Life Playing Center Field for the Cubs

Michael Leach

When I was a kid in the 1950s, that's all I wanted to be: center fielder for the Cubs.

My preparation was playing catch in an alley behind our apartment on Addison Street, three blocks away from the ballpark. Tommy Lentzen threw balls to my left, my right, in front of my feet, above my head, and I learned to catch them all, even soaring above the gutter for the ones he lofted above garage roofs. I learned to hit by playing "fast pitching" in a school yard with a square chalked on the wall for a strike zone and a tennis ball for a league ball. When I was thirteen I tried out for a Pony League team on a field two bus rides away that had a fence and seats. The coach hit balls at me in center, and despite a leaping grab of a liner while on the run and a bullet throw from center to home I didn't make the cut. When it came time for me to hit, I found that a tennis ball was as different from a hard ball as a suction-cup dart was from a guided missile.

When I wasn't playing catch in the alley, I was playing softball with the other street urchins on the corner of Lakewood and Eddy Streets. The manhole covers were bases, and we played all summer with the same old ball until it was as soft as a pillow. Even so, you'd better not smack it too far down the middle or it might crack the window of an apartment building. You had to pull the ball to the street on the left or punch it down the street to the right. You began playing after school and didn't stop until your mother called your name from a wooden porch or the setting sun painted the windows gold and the streets turned dark.

Legend has it that my father took me to my first Cubs game when I was a week old. He pushed the buggy up the ramp to the top of the bleachers in left center, charmed a sweet old lady to baby sit me so he could join Uncle Charlie and his pals down in the first row and drink beer and hoot and howl and maybe catch a homer. I had a perfect view from my perch and plenty of time to survey the territory for when my time came to play center field for the Cubs.

Our one-bedroom apartment faced Addison Street. At 11 o'clock I looked out the window at the happy people parading toward the park to watch batting practice before the game. In those days our neighborhood was not called Wrigleyville but Lakeview, a working-class neighborhood where summer days were for swimming in Lake Michigan or going to Cubs Park, that's what we called it, because it was a *park*. It wasn't winning that drew us, that was not going to happen much; it was hanging out on *this day* with nice people under the sun with a lake breeze cooling our faces, and making happy talk as we washed down ten-cent hot dogs with five-cent Cokes and cheered on our "lovable losers" for three hours that seemed like one. That's why Ernie Banks used to say, "It's a beautiful day! Let's play two!"

Ernie played for the love of the game. He was like the Zen master who said, "Children get to heaven by playing." Ernie was in heaven between third and second base. Like his friend and my other hero, Willie Mays of the Giants, Ernie Banks loved being alive.

My second favorite team was the Brooklyn Dodgers. One day after a game I stole down to the Dodger dugout to see if a player would give me a used ball. This day Carl Furillo, their tough right fielder who wore a 12 o'clock shadow that made him look like a villain out of a Dick Tracy comic, was rubbing his glove with oil.

"Hey, Carl, great game! You wouldn't have any balls that are no good, would you?"

Carl smiled. He knew the routine. He picked up a Louisville Slugger bat that had a tiny crack near the knob and said, "How about this instead?"

It was his bat. He had used it today. He couldn't use it again. I would use it for the next twenty years.

I taped the crack with black adhesive and swung it that summer hundreds of times a day, shredding tennis ball after tennis ball when we played fast pitching. I tried to use it when my turn came to hit at the Pony League tryout. The coach said no, it's too big. I had to use one of their aluminum bats. It was like trying to smack frozen meatballs with a breadstick. "Sorry, kid." It was on that afternoon that my dream to play center field for the Cubs almost died.

Cubs Park was my open-air basilica but St. Andrew's was my neighborhood church and I also wanted to be a priest like Fr. Jack Gorman, who had a great jump shot. So that September I went to Quigley Preparatory Seminary.

When I was seventeen Johnny Pritcher and I took the el train from Quigley to Wrigley after school to sneak into the park for the end of the game. The Cubs had lost nine in a row and were in last place. After the game a handful of players stayed for batting practice. Johnny and I made our way to the dugout and asked coach Dutch Leonard if we could shag flies.

"Sorry, kids, you might get hurt."

"Aw c'mon, Dutch, we won't get hurt. We got our gloves. *Please*."

"What the hell. Go ahead. Be careful."

Johnny went to short, and I went to center. A line drive whistled past his ear, almost ripped his head off. I was hanging out with a couple of rookies in an outfield I had first mapped out at one week old. This was my chance. *Mike Leach, at center field for the Chicago Cubs!* I'd prove myself! I'd do something spectacular! I'd made sensational catches of a hard ball in the alley a million times!

Crack! A towering fly soared toward the sky. My inner GPS saw it dropping just in front of the ivy.

"I got it! I got it!" I pedaled backward. I'd make a basket catch like Willie Mays. I bumped into Moe Drabowsky. The ball landed just behind his head.

"What's the matter with you, kid?"

"I thought I got it. . . . I'm sorry."

I picked the ball up. I had one more chance. I wound up and took a couple steps forward and threw that ball with all my might to home plate. I'd make it on a bullet just like I did at Pony League.

The ball almost made it to second.

On a roll.

My soul learned a lesson in humility that day. Being a star isn't happiness. Ernie Banks was a star but always knew what I had known in the alley and on Eddy Street and then forgot: the love of being alive and the joy of just playing.

Baseball, like life, sets you free only when you play it for fun.

JULY 15, 2016

✧ SIGHTING ✧

I'm not a smart man but I know what love is.

—FORREST GUMP

God is love, and those who abide in love abide in God, and God abides in them. . . . The commandment we have from him is this: those who love God must love their brothers and sisters also.

—1 JOHN: 4:16, 21

30

The Hands We Hold Are Gifts

Ginny Kubitz Moyer

I was sitting at my prayer desk the other night, two flickering candles in front of me, letting my mind wander as I looked at the small framed icon of Our Lady of Perpetual Help that once belonged to my grandmother. It's an inexpensive framed image, one that she must have had since the 1960s at least, but in the candlelight it shone like pure gold. And as I looked at it—a picture I see every single day—I noticed something. For the first time, I realized that Mary and Jesus were holding hands.

That moved me.

I'm forever reminding my kids to hold my hand. Any time we're in a parking lot or crossing a street, it comes out of my mouth automatically: "Hold my hand." And the boy in question slips a sticky damp little hand in mine, and off we go (unless it's Luke, my little Daddy's boy, who invariably says, "No! I want to hold Daddy's hand!" and runs over to Scott).

I feel far more comfortable walking out in public that way, although the terrifying reality is that in a parking lot with huge cars backing out and turning corners, joined hands can only keep you so safe. But still, it's something. And it always moves me when I don't have to say it, when the boys automatically reach for my hand as we cross a street.

They won't do that forever, I know. Give them about ten years, and they'll probably be about as likely to touch my hand in public as they would be to touch a hot stove. But for now, I love it that Matthew, my big kindergartner with a backpack and homework and serious responsibilities as Table Captain in his classroom, instinctively slides his hand into mine, knowing that I will always want to hold it.

All this floated through my mind there at my prayer desk, at 11:00 on a Saturday night, as Mary and Jesus glowed in the flickering light. And then I returned to my book of prayers (I was praying the Liturgy of the Hours), and I read Jesus's words on the cross: "Into your hands I commend my spirit."

Hands again, I thought to myself. This time it's not about holding hands, but about placing yourself in someone else's.

Then I looked at the little statue of Mary, the one that I bought in Lourdes in 2002.

I thought about how perfectly her gesture—those hands extended, palms out—captures the sentiment of Christ's

words. Into your hands I commend my spirit. It's a gesture
of surrender, a gesture that says, You can use these hands
for whatever you need. That's what Mary did in agreeing
to become the mother of the Savior. She made the tacit
promise that those hands of hers would be there to hold
her son's hand in all seasons and in all things. Even when
he got mature enough to venture off without her, those
hands would always be there anytime he needed the tangible assurance that he was not alone.

And as my mind drifted in and out, I remembered a
time when Luke was two and a half. He was adorable at
two, but he could also be ever so challenging and ever
so independent. We were sitting in a taxi, all four of us,
en route to the airport to take a red-eye to Florida to visit
Scott's parents. It was a Friday evening, and I sat wedged
next to Luke's car seat, thinking about the five-hour flight
ahead of us and the hassle of getting two sleepy boys and
two car seats and one stroller and various suitcases through
an airport and onto a plane and later through another airport and to a rental car terminal and thence to a hotel. And
I sat there in the taxi, for a brief moment with nothing to
do, bracing myself for the big evening ahead.

And suddenly, without saying anything, Luke reached
out his hand and took mine. With that gesture my mind
quieted and my soul began to see. I held his sweet little
hand and stroked it and watched the hotels flash past on
the freeway and thought: This moment is a gift. This moment in time is precious to me.

There's a lot in parenting that feels out of my hands. That's true for all of us, I suspect. But when one of my boys slips a sticky little hand into mine, I can't help but feel, in some very deep and visceral way, that all is well.

MAY 24, 2013

31

Holy Biscuits in Ethiopia

Miriam Therese Winter

It was barely midday, and I was already exhausted. We had set up this makeshift feeding center in Ethiopia for victims of a devastating famine, and they now blanketed the room. Women cradling emaciated children pressed against one another, as each claimed a coveted piece of that hard mud floor.

I was about to assist the nurses attending a dying baby when one of our Ethiopian aides burst into the room. "Come!" she shouted. "Hurry! They are calling for a doctor. They say there is a dead body beyond the outer wall."

We had no doctors.

Preoccupied with the emergencies at hand, one nurse said to her: "If he's dead, he doesn't need a doctor. Can't you see? We are busy here."

The aide persisted. "Someone must certify that the person is dead before they can proceed with a burial. It is our tradition. It must be done before the sun goes down."

"You go," the head nurse said to me.

"I can't do that," I said. "I'm not qualified."

"Dead is dead," she said. "Surely you can handle that. Go make the official pronouncement."

So Dr. Winter, PhD in liturgical studies, followed the Ethiopian aide, feeling as ill at ease as a freshman en route to a qualifying exam.

The body was a long way off, on a sandy beach by a river's edge, where a very large crowd was waiting. All of them were male. When they saw me, they began to shout in a language I did not understand. Warning signals went off within me. I'm in the middle of nowhere. Nobody knows I am here. We two are the only women in the midst of a hostile mob.

"Why are they so angry?" I asked my companion. "Why are they angry with me?"

One of the men responded, "We are angry because you up there in that camp are the ones who killed this man. Yesterday, he came to beg for food, and you turned him away. Now he has died of hunger, and he died because of you."

I had to calm this volatile situation. I said, "Let us first be certain he is dead. Then we can investigate why." They agreed. I approached the body baking in the sun.

As I stood there, staring death in the face, I recognized who the one looking up at me through his unseeing eyes was, and I was horrified. A young adult male, stick thin, in rags, had indeed come into the compound yesterday, saying he was hungry. He pleaded for a box of biscuits, that staple of intensive feeding centers everywhere. I was about to give it to him when a staff member berated me: "Those biscuits are for the children. There won't be enough if you start giving them to whoever comes along." Then she said sharply to the starving man: "Why did you come here? You know you are not allowed. This camp is only for children and those biscuits are for them."

After she left, I took a biscuit and placed it in the man's hand.

I barely slept at all that night, for my heart had been filled with remorse. Now the source of my guilt and regret had returned in death, but our status was reversed. He was secure in the embrace of Allah, and I was in need of deliverance.

I prayed for divine guidance and then said to the mob: "This man is indeed dead, but he did not die of hunger. Look, a piece of uneaten biscuit, which I had given to him yesterday, is still there in his hand." He was indeed clutching that life-giving bread in his lifeless hand. A murmur of appreciation arose and spilled over into prayer. After the young man's body had been wrapped in a clean new cloth, something amazing happened: A beautiful butterfly—the first I had seen in Ethiopia in all the times I had been there—circled the dead man's body, settled briefly on the cloth that covered his forehead, and then flew away, circling, spiraling upward, until it disappeared.

I saw something invisible but real through the eye of my soul.

Living among the disenfranchised had transformed my perspective. I would never look at religion and society or my own faith traditions in the same way again. I saw more than ever that the spirit of the living God inhabits all creation, even biscuits and butterflies, the living and the dead. When we see life in this way, we behold the secular as sacred, the "other" as part of our self and of one another, and we welcome the outsider in. Any meal that nourishes both body and spirit is a eucharist with a small "e" and potentially transformative to one with eyes to see.

The spirit of God, the spirit of Jesus, earth's spirit, our spirit, is all one spirit.

You, I, we, and they, are no more.

This is what I was graced to see in Ethiopia.

APRIL 27, 2012

32

Christ and Cerebral Palsy

Michael Leach

How easy it is to see the face of Christ in the eyes of a baby or the limbs of a child racing a kite or the features of a movie star. The key to eternal life is to behold the loveliness of Christ in the eyes of a child born blind, the limbs of a teenager with cerebral palsy, the features of a woman scarred with burns. The truth is—the beauty is—each wears the face of Christ, and they all play as one.

How many times have I averted my eyes from a picture in *Time* of a starving baby with flies on its face or haven't paid attention to the fellow slumped over in a wheelchair at a wedding or found an excuse not to visit a friend wasting away with cancer or pretended the family at the diner who had a noisy child didn't exist? And what a blessing it becomes to begin to see with spiritual eyes and behold the image of the emaciated baby as she really is, *whole*; to touch the cripple in the wheelchair and say hello; to visit a friend or acquaintance in the hospital or nursing home with a great big smile; and simply to see the mother and father with the overactive child as the family of God they really are. The truth is—the wonder is—that the words of Christ are literally true: "whatever you do unto these, you do for me." And what we do for Christ we do for them and for ourselves and for the whole human race. For all of us, each of us, are one.

The new science of metapsychiatry validates this teaching by demonstrating that we all have a spiritual faculty to enter a rehab room and see Christ, to help a homeless woman push her shopping cart across the street and know that the story of St. Christopher is the story of us all. Metapsychiatry calls this ability to realize what is really before our eyes the faculty of beholding. Beholding is a higher faculty than the intellect or imagination or intuition, but one we have not been taught to cultivate. To behold is to see the invisible (what is real and lasting) in the visible (what appears and disappears). St. Paul teaches: "We do not lose heart. Even though our outer nature is wasting away, our inner nature is being renewed day by day. . . . We look not at what can be seen but at what cannot be seen; for what can be seen is temporary, but what cannot be seen is eternal" (2 Cor 4:16, 18).

Psychiatrist Thomas Hora (1914–95), who founded metapsychiatry upon the teachings of Jesus and spiritual learnings from other religions as well as psychiatry, writes:

> There is more to man than meets the eye. We all have the faculty to discern spiritual qualities in the world. We can see honesty; we can see integrity; we can see beauty; we can see love; we can see goodness; we

can see joy; we can see peace; we can see harmony; we can see intelligence; and so forth. None of these things has any form; none of these things can be imagined; none of these things is tangible, and yet they can be seen. What is the organ that sees these invisible things? Some people call it the soul, spirit, or consciousness. Man is a spiritual being endowed with spiritual faculties of perception.

Each of us can behold the truth of being in all of us.

Prayer

Jesus, the next time I see someone with what doctors call cerebral palsy or Down Syndrome, grace me with the sight to realize what is really there: goodness, innocence, love, joy, intelligence, and abundant beauty. You embraced lepers and felt purity and the scales fell from their faces. Help me to know, right now: when I look at anyone I am looking my Self, I am looking at you, for all of us, each of us, is a spiritual aspect of you and only you! God bless everyone! I close my eyes now and remember someone I've passed by or ignored and ask you to see love for me. I am learning that I can behold you and everyone with the same eyes that you behold us. I am going to sit still now and listen . . . and see.

Thank you, Jesus. I have to go now and call someone up or maybe go to the hospital.

NOVEMBER 11, 2011

33

God Rides the R Train

James Behrens

In him we live and move and have our being in God.

—ACTS 17:28

God is love.

—1 JOHN 4:8

We live and ride and have our being in Love.

On my last trip up North, I rode the New York subways a lot. My aunt was in a Brooklyn hospital, and the easiest way to get there was by taking the train from New Jersey and then walking a few blocks from Penn Station to catch the R subway to Brooklyn. All in all, it took about an hour and a half to get from New Jersey to Brooklyn.

I like the subways.

I was thinking about the people I saw on them as I was falling off to sleep last night. Maybe that is a kind of prayer for them. I hope so. I realize prayer is supposed to go directly to God with no stops or detours. But the subway train and its riders were on my mind last night. The people almost swayed in my thoughts as I pictured them riding the rails beneath Manhattan. So I caught another ride with them, and I think that is close to God, too. For God must have been in the subway, too.

There was a Chinese man whose little daughter squeezed in between his legs. He sat next to me, by the door. His daughter looked up at him and pointed to a plastic bottle he held in his hands. She wanted a drink, and he would smile and slip the straw in her mouth. She would finish drinking and then rest her head in his lap. She looked at me and smiled.

A young Latina mother sat across from me. Her little boy, who looked to be about five, couldn't stay still. He would run from her, and then turn and laugh, and then run back. She would try to grab him but he was quick. He'd be off again before she could get her hands on him. I had the feeling that the boy would have been in big trouble had not the others on the car been looking on. The mother was careful to keep her cool. And the little boy knew it. He loved it. And exploited it.

A young black couple were holding hands and kissing.

A lot of people had iPods, iPads, Kindles, MP3 players, and other devices that had games on them. In fact, I would say most people were absorbed in those things.

One lady sat across from me, and when I looked at her, I had to look away because I could not tell if she was a man or a woman and didn't want to stare. There was something about her or him that was vaguely undefined. Hard to tell sometimes.

And old Chinese man was reading his paper. The paper was in Chinese, and I could see a page from how he held the paper. I think it takes a near genius to read Chinese. He smiled as he was reading. And I wondered what made him smile.

A young guy got on with a CD player and his buddy was right behind him. When the train started to move, the guy turned on the music and the buddy started to dance and twist, and then got onto the floor and spun around and around. The music was good—I think it was something about sex by James Brown. It was a fast, popping kind of song that made me want to move, to dance. But as it was, I sat there.

The more I write this, the more I remember. All the people, so handsome and beautiful, living life as best they can and moving beneath one of the greatest cities in the world. All of it made by God, though God is always discreet, hidden, living as he does in all living things. In the dance, in little thirsty babies, in kids running up and down the aisles, in the smile of an old man and the kiss of the young. It is there every second of every day. They say Manhattan is a city that never sleeps.

God doesn't sleep, either. God rides.

MARCH 16, 2012

✧ SIGHTING ✧

Every moment comes to us with a command from God, only to pass on and plunge into eternity, there to remain forever what we made of it.

—ST. FRANCIS DE SALES

34

An Unexpected Gift of Chronic Illness

Teresa Rhodes

I was lying half naked and tethered to an EKG machine. To my distress, the technician sighed. I asked if there was something wrong and she said: "You are fine, but last week my mother-in-law died in Bangladesh, and I couldn't go home for the funeral. I've had no time to mourn." The computer traced my cardiac rhythms as she described the depth of her grief in an unexpected meeting of our hearts. As I was leaving she said, "Thank you for listening. Please pray for me."

I remembered her in the long days of surgical recovery that I now call "going on retreat." I've had many orthopedic surgeries to correct painful deformities caused by two decades of rheumatoid arthritis. The stillness required for bones and metal plates to grow together creates space for me to pray, carried as I am on the grace of other people's kindness. I have lots of time to read and meditate from a level of vulnerability and dependence that is essential to healing. Yet the gift of those days—and I dare say of a chronic illness itself—is the constant opportunity to heed the words of Isaiah: "Listen that you might live."

Much of my professional life was devoted to active listening. I traveled the world as the director of international HR/operations for a human rights organization, listening to stories and concerns, confident that I could figure things out, or failing that, push through difficulty. I do not give up easily, a stubborn resolve that has served me well in life even as it has, on more than one occasion, overtaken good sense. I brought that force of will to my illness, pushing through pain, fatigue, and medication side effects long past the point that was reasonable. But a hospitalization three years ago led me to understand that not listening to the vulnerabilities of my own illness is life threatening, something my doctor had been saying for some time. I knew for years that the nature of rheumatoid arthritis could cause a sudden change in my ability to navigate the world, and of course I believed I could outrun it. Assumptions of control and invulnerability have a powerful way of drowning out the truth.

After I left the hospital, I went on a sick leave with hope that I would get better. When it was clear that I was living a new phase of the disease, I made the painful decision to leave the work I loved. The day I signed the resignation papers, I put away my well-stamped passport and with it all my anticipated journeys. I donated my business suits and briefcases to a program that provides work clothes to women in transition. I discovered how much I depended on my professional identity when it was suddenly gone, and with it, the scaffolding of my days. I did not know quite what to do with myself, especially because I did not, and do not, have the energy to undertake all the projects that live in the back of my mind. The most daunting aspect of the transition is that what I considered my best stuff—self-defining strength, determination, and hard work—are not only useless but could do me harm. Sooner or later we all find ourselves in this kind of impasse where past resources, points of identity, and strengths are no longer available or helpful. It takes time and patience to listen to the emptiness long enough to know that what feels like loss is the energy of conversion.

I am discovering the contours of that conversion as I learn to differentiate birds' songs and hear the words of scripture with an embodied appreciation of the great reversals that are at the heart of the gospel. I am amazed what people tell me in the course of the day, how often I am asked to pray for someone, and how delightful it is to do so without the pressure of time.

Listening from brokenness becomes its own strength because although we come to it on different paths, our shared humanity guarantees the experience of painful limits and unchosen loss. I am about to begin another eight-week retreat, a sacred opportunity to hear and tend the cry for healing we all carry in our bones. To do so has become my unexpected vocation.

SEPTEMBER 27, 2013

35

Angels in the Radiation Lab

Claire Bangasser

I read an essay in the spirituality journal *Sacred Space* by a woman who sees God's presence in the oncology ward where she works. It reminded me of the times I spent in a radiation lab after my breast cancer operation. I'll always remember the kindness of the nurses, how gently they treated me. They moved around like angels who had chosen to become human for those of us who needed them.

I learned to use my radiation time to pray for those I did not like, for those who had hurt me, to be an angel to them as the nurses were to me. My prayer began as I passed through the lab doors and descended to the basement where the radiation took place. I sat in a windowless room where other patients also looked at their thoughts and waited their turn. When my turn came I paced into the radiation room, lay down on a slab under a huge light, and let the nurse arrange me so the rays would hit the fresh scar on my breast like a laser beam in a James Bond movie. I was left alone with the buzzing machine, and I prayed for those whom I had let break my peace over the years. Those quiet moments felt like a direct line to God.

I came to this kind of praying first by the grace of wisdom, and later, more profoundly, through suffering.

Before my diagnosis of cancer I had an inspiration to revisit Taizé, the monastic prayer community two hours from where I was staying in France.

Like Samuel, who had been called to visit Eli to learn what to do with his life, I had been listening for God's voice to tell me for a long time but hearing only silence. So I decided to drive to Taizé and leave a note in the prayer box: "Here I am, Lord. What can I do for you?" A few days later I heard the "still, small voice" asking me to pray for others. Mine would be a ministry of intercession.

Then cancer barged into my life, seizing center stage, scaring me out of my wits. Thoughts of the future were like coming attractions for a horror movie. Suddenly I could make no plans. At first I fantasized I'd just go to the hospital in the morning, have the cancer removed, and go home fine in the evening. My surgeon said: "It's not a cold you have, Claire. It's cancer. Face it, or it will not let you go."

How does one face cancer?

It was cancer that faced me after the operation. I was in my hospital bed waiting for the results, wondering whether metastases had multiplied under my armpits. How bad was it really? Would I need chemotherapy? Would there be years of suffering?

That night I stayed awake in the dark. On a similar occasion a friend had experienced a luminous encounter with Christ, which filled her with hope and joy. I had just the opposite experience. I had always imagined that the day I'd die, I would behold a basket of flowers representing all the good things I had done in my life. That night I found my basket empty, like the tracks of clear-cutting I discovered the first time I visited the Pacific Northwest.

In the darkness of my room I could hear and feel only my beating heart. And I realized from my depth: "Oh, even my heart is not mine, God! It is really yours. I have nothing I can call my own." That was a moment when angels spoke for me.

Before returning home I learned that my cancer had not spread, that I would only need radiation therapy and a single drug. God was giving me a second chance. How grateful I felt then! I rushed to confession and told my priest all that I had discovered that night of dread.

And I asked: How does one repair broken relationships? How does one fix a life? I began to know: everyone is called to a ministry of intercession.

Cancer was a changing agent in my life. It was as if a part of me had died on the operating table, poisonous pieces of anger being surgically removed from my heart and goodness injected in their place.

My prayers for others in the radiation lab were just a beginning. It still is not easy for me to forgive, to let go, to move on. I need to do it "seventy times seven" times, as Jesus counseled. I need all the time that is left to me and won't waste one day. My life is no longer the wasteland it once was. It is a radiation room filled with angels. For this I am infinitely grateful.

AUGUST 3, 2012

36

I Know There Will Always Be Kindness

Michael Leach

I pick up Vickie from adult day care and drive to Chipotle for takeout. We park in the handicapped space in front. A young African American in an apron rushes out the door and holds it open for us. "Mister, I want to show you something," he says. "I have a son!"

"That's wonderful, Andre!"

Andre escorts us to the counter and runs to the back for his cell phone.

Molly with the Smiling Blue Eyes stands over the food. "Let me guess," she says. "White rice, pinto beans, chicken, just a little hot sauce on both."

"I'm proud of you, Molly. Your mom must be very proud."

She loads up both plates. Vickie squeezes herself against my back, her arms wrapped around my chest, her head resting on my back like a child as we toddle alongside the counter. This sight kills people. They can't take it. They want to feed us.

Jeter as in Derek Jeter (that's what I call him because he's a Yankee fan) is at the cash register. We talk about the World Series. Molly passes over the bag, and I hand him a twenty. "No charge," Jeter says.

The manager Justin, who knows every customer, started comping us about six months ago. Not every time or even a lot of times but enough times to make me wonder if my old-man pants (baggy blue with a drawstring) and the same old Cubs T-shirt makes me look rundown. Jeter says it's policy not to charge good customers every now and then, but frankly, I think it's the Mike and Vickie Shuffle. Certainly kindness shines through their gesture in choosing us.

And it's not just Chipotle people who are kind to us.

Abdul at Boston Chicken sometimes gives us two platters of turkey for the price of one and always slips a free slice of apple pie in the bag.

Michael, the manager of Bull's Head Diner in Stamford, likes to stuff a free brownie, the size of a brick, into our bag. Gabriel the archangel, a waiter who has been at the diner since we started going there twenty years ago, carries our bag to the car and opens the door for Vickie and always asks about our grandkids and we ask him about his family, and his mother in Mexico has made it through the earthquake you'll be happy to know.

The Dalai Lama once counseled followers to be kind whenever and however possible. "And it is always possible," he added.

"Don't go yet!" Andre catches up to us before we leave Chipotle. "Look," he says and hands me his cell phone.

"He's beautiful!" I say. "Look at those chubby cheeks! What's his name?"

"Amir."

"A great name. You have other kids?"

"My first son, his name is Andre like me. He's four."

"I remember when our grandkids were four. That's a fun age. I'm putting you and Lil' Andre and Amir in my prayers, right up here where I pray all the time."

"Thank you. I'm praying for you, Mister."

I wave at the kids behind the counter. "Thanks, guys!"

The Chiptoleans wave, even the ones chopping pork and slicing steak and boiling rice that steams up into their faces like heady incense.

We pull into our driveway. A white plastic bag hangs on the doorknob. Fresh tomatoes, big ones, little ones, some as red as the Chipotle logo, others yellow as custard. No note. Just the tomatoes. Sometimes I think people are conspiring to feed us.

I suspect the Tomato Fairy is Terry Kutzen, one of Vickie's golfing pals from the old days who stays in touch. Whenever it's suppertime and I don't know what to get, Terry calls up out of the blue and says, "I just made meat loaf and got plenty left. It's hot and ready to go. Can I come over?" If it's not her meat loaf, it's her chicken with herbs and spices from the Far East or plastic containers of magical chicken soup that could cure lower back pain and it's always enough for three full meals.

The Tomato Fairy also could have been Darlene from around the corner whose husband had Alzheimer's, too,

and died three years ago, and who bakes more variet-
ies of cookies than Famous Amos. Or maybe it's Helen
from down the block, who every now and then appears
bearing cellophane-wrapped platters with a three-course
gourmet meal or, better yet, a paper plate overflowing
with lip-burning chocolate chippers just out of the oven.
Or it could be Sibley next door, who calls and says, "I just
tried something new. Would you like to try it?" Before she
moved to Florida it was Jane, who specialized in roast beef
that would slice itself as your eyes slobbered over it. And
it's always our son Chris's great big Heart of a girlfriend
Jessica who cooks all-day dinners for our whole family, on
Thanksgiving and Christmas and any old Sunday at all, at
our house or theirs, and even takes the lead in cleaning the
dishes. I tell you: people will always be kind.

Vickie and I can afford to eat at our diner every night,
but nothing tastes as good as the kindness that carries our
bag to the car or opens the door for us at Chipotle or hangs
a plastic bag of just-picked tomatoes on our doorknob.

Yes, it's a big bad world out there, but after every earthquake we watch men and women clawing through rocks to
save children, for every hurricane we see neighbors helping
neighbors and strangers in other lands sending cans of food
through their churches, and for every Las Vegas or Sandy
Hook we behold people standing in line at hospitals to
donate precious blood. And for every klutz like me who
cares for a Vickie and can only cook Campbell's soup, there
are always, always, Tomato Fairies.

NOVEMBER 4, 2017

37

It All Tastes Like Love

Fran Rossi Szpylczyn

Jennie and Darlene are arranging name tags on a folding table in front of the church. "Be my first?" I ask them. Mom and daughter beam. I take my first picture on this special day at the Church of the Immaculate Conception in Glenville, New York. I'm Fran, the church office manager. It's a madcap job, but somebody's got to do it.

I snap a nursing-home van as it pulls to the curb. Joan and Pam help old folks in wheelchairs move down the lift as if they were all on a children's ride at the parish carnival. Father Jerry in a white chasuble comes out to greet them. Everyone is as expectant as the biblical Elizabeth when she greeted the young Mary. I click away like Diane Arbus in a sunny mood. The elderly and infirm, along with anyone who wants to be healed, are here to be blessed.

Our twice-yearly anointing mass will soon begin.

I take a long shot of the Explorers, Jettas, and Corollas lined up politely in the parking lot like ambassadors from the United Nations. I snap Rachel, the pastoral-care director and coordinator of the event, as she embraces our elderly Mary, whose coat is as pink as cotton candy. Other greeters stand at the curb of the church and share hugs and handshakes and hand out worship aids. My camera captures the young and the old, the fit and the feeble, the happy and the weary. I hope the photos will form a collage of one body of Christ: a portrait of bodies and souls, broken and whole, immaculately reconceived and remembered in this church on this day. No one will be ignored, left out, or cast aside. The entire body will know that whatever happens to one of them happens to all of them, and that what happens to all happens to each.

I blend with the others inside the church and take a picture of the widow Jan who treads up the aisle. Her eyesight is failing, but she is determined. Helping her into a pew, I introduce her to Bob and Eileen, a couple who always manifests cheerfulness despite life's challenges. A photo of these three will show the beautiful unity in the diversity of our parish body.

The procession begins. The congregation sings as one: "Gather us in, the blind and the lame!" Gnarled and shaking hands make the sign of the cross as the liturgy begins. Everyone listens. We are like children at story time. We hear scripture passages about healing that assure us of the promise of Christ.

When it's time for the anointing, Father Jerry approaches a row of wheelchairs parked in front of the altar. He bows, anointing each person with chrism. A man in his eighties weeps; his aid daubs at his tears with a tissue.

I pray that my camera captures the compassion I see with my soul.

Fathers Jerry and Leo move from pew to pew, bearing oil and blessings. Leo anoints Rose, her eyes closed, her up-turned palms extended in a gesture of giving and receiving. Ed is so tall that Jerry must reach up to him. His wife, Ann, is the opposite, and Jerry smiles as he stoops to anoint her.

I put down my camera. Father Jerry's thumb marks a cross on my forehead. When he blesses my palms, the pressure of the crosses traced into each one makes me feel woozy. Without my camera to protect me, I feel vulnerable. I am broken, too. My legs and arms work, my eyes focus, there is no arthritis in my hands, but I need healing, too.

"Go in peace to love and serve the Lord!"

I follow everyone to the parish hall for another kind of banquet. Fran, Anne, and other parish nurses have put out a feast of egg, chicken, and tuna salad sandwiches. It all tastes like love.

The soundtrack of a community in delight spreads through the room as everyone eats and talks. Father Jerry moves from table to table, leaving a wake of contentment. My camera clicks away as he chats with a spry and playful Clara. Emily, who knits us slippers, listens in, and I photo-graph her, too. Senior citizen George is with Father Leo, but he turns his head to smile into my lens like George Clooney as I walk by. I feel like a cameraman in a Fellini movie. The sounds of heaven on earth fill the room with joyful noise.

We depart greater than when we arrived. We are the body of Christ, broken and restored, dying and rising, reconceived and remembered, here and now, once and forever.

AUGUST 31, 2012

✦ SIGHTING ✦

The Little Prince Tells You a Secret

And now here is my secret, a very simple secret: It is only with the heart that one can see rightly; what is essential is invisible to the eye.

—ANTOINE DE SAINT-EXUPÉRY,
THE LITTLE PRINCE

PART THREE

FORGIVENESS

Be kind and compassionate to one another, forgiving each other, just as in Christ God forgives you.

—EPHESIANS 4:32

There is no love without forgiveness, and there is no forgiveness without love.

—BRYANT H. MCGILL

38

The Day I Stood Shimmering in Shame

Brian Doyle

Committed a sin yesterday, in the hallway, at noon. I roared at my son, I grabbed him by the shirt collar, I frightened him so badly that he cowered and wept, and when he turned to run, I grabbed him by the arm so roughly that he flinched, and it was that flicker of fear and pain across his face, the bright eager holy riveting face I have loved for ten years, that stopped me then and haunts me this morning; for I am the father of his fear, I sent it snarling into his heart, and I can never get it out now, which torments me.

Yes, he was picking on his brother, and yes, he had picked on his brother all morning, and yes, this was the culmination of many edgy incidents already, and no, he hadn't paid the slightest attention to warnings and remonstrations and fulminations, and yes, he had been snide and supercilious all day, and yes, he had deliberately done exactly the thing he had specifically been warned not to do, for murky reasons, but still, I roared at him and grabbed him and terrified him and made him cower, and now there is a dark evil wriggle between us that makes me sit here with my hands over my face, ashamed to the bottom of my bones.

I do not know how sins can be forgiven. I grasp the concept, I admire the genius of the idea, I suspect it to be the seed of all real peace, I savor the Tutus and Gandhis who have the mad courage to live by it, but I do not understand how foul can be made fair. What is done cannot be undone, and my moment of rage in the hallway is an indelible scar on his heart and mine, and while my heart is a ragged old bag after nearly half a century of slings and stings, his is still new, eager, open, suggestible, innocent; he has committed only the small sins of a child, the halting first lies, the failed test paper hidden in the closet, the window broken in petulance, the stolen candy bar, the silent witness as a classmate is bullied, the insults flung like bitter knives.

Whereas I am a man, and have had many lies squirming in my mouth, and have committed calumny, and far too often evaded the mad ragged Christ, ignored his stink, his rotten teeth, his cloak of soggy newspapers, his voice of broken glass.

No god can forgive what we do to each other; only the injured can summon that extraordinary grace, and where such grace is born we cannot say, for all our fitful genius and miraculous machinery. We use the word *god* so easily, so casually, as if our label for the incomprehensible meant anything at all; and we forget all too easily that the wriggle of holy is born only through the stammer and stumble of us, who are always children. So we turn again and again to each other, and bow, and ask forgiveness, and mill what mercy we can muster from the muddle of our hearts.

The instant I let go of my son's sinewy arm in the hallway, he sprinted away and slammed the door and flew off the porch and ran down the street, and I stood there simmering in shame. Then I walked down the hill into the laurel thicket as dense and silent as the dawn of the world and found him there huddled and sobbing. We sat in the moist green dark for a long time, not saying anything, the branches burly and patient. Finally, I asked quietly for his forgiveness and he asked for mine and we walked out of the woods hand in hand, changed men.

JANUARY 17, 2014

39

The Gift of Being Brought to Our Knees and Forgiven for Our Sins

Heather King

> *The eyes of peacemakers are watchful, caring eyes and their fellow wayfarers find warmth in them like people at the fireside. They never find a motive for fighting because they know that they are only accountable for peace and peace is not preserved by battles.*
>
> *They know that dividing a single atom can unleash cosmic warfare.*
>
> *They also know that there is a chain that links human beings together and that when one human cell is torn by anger, jealousy, or bitterness, the reaction of war can rebound to the end of the universe.*
>
> —Servant of God Madeleine Delbrêl

One of the most significant ramifications of the crucifixion is that Christ died not *in the course of* committing violence, but *instead of* committing violence.

I'm among the first to decry the violence of weapons and war.

But, of course, there are ways of committing violence other than with weapons. There is the violence of anger, of self-pity, of pride. There's the violence of, say, adultery.

In fact, my first inkling of the concept of the Mystical Body came to me when I got sober in 1987 and did a moral inventory around my life in the bars. That was when it first dawned on me that when I had slept with a married man, that had affected his wife, whether or not she ever "knew." It affected the guy's kids, if he had kids, whether or not they ever "knew." It affected the guy, and in some way everyone he came in contact with.

Later would come the gut-wrenching knowledge of the terrible violence, the sorrow, the tear to the human fabric of abortion. Later would come years of bearing the wound of my own three abortions in silence. Later I would see how the violence I'd inflicted upon my unborn children and myself spilled over into all my human relationships: in a tendency to dominate on the one hand, and to be overly dependent on the other; a tendency toward romantic obsession, a form of lust.

That's why to be brought to our knees by our sicknesses, our sin, is such a great gift. No one is more fervent, or more grateful, than the criminal who's been welcomed back to the banquet table. No one is more willing to walk through the world unarmed. "They" might kill you—they killed Christ—but in being forgiven, and in forgiving ourselves, we're freed from the bondage of fear. We're free to live out the rest of our days in love. We're free to answer Christ's call to be peacemakers.

To travel about unarmed is folly in the eyes of the world. But "my kingdom is not of this world," said Christ, who himself walked unarmed among criminals of every sort.

If I really want to be a peacemaker, I have to come back again and again to the terrible violence I've committed myself. I'm called to a constant examination of conscience, to penance, to sacrifice.

That's one reason why, for years, I've been going once a month with some fellow sober drunks to an LA-area jail.

One night especially stands out. As usual, we could bring in nothing but ID and our car keys. As usual, we had to wait for an escort to our assigned pod. As usual, we walked down labyrinthine halls, through a few steel-reinforced sally ports, and past several inmates who'd been instructed to stand head to wall with their hands clasped behind them. As usual, the air was thick with the smell of bad food, unwashed bodies, fear.

Still, pill call wasn't *so* loud this particular evening that we literally had to shout, which is often the case. The inmates were attentive, which, since many of them were mentally ill and/or highly medicated, was also exceptional.

We told our stories. The guys had a chance to ask questions. One hollow-eyed guy with dreadlocks and a missing front tooth said, "I killed someone in a drunk-driving accident. I just got thirty-five years." Another jittery kid offered, "I don't think I'm an addict. I just make really bad decisions when I'm high."

As usual, the inmates gave us way more than we gave them. As usual, those of us who were going to get to leave and those who were staying inside bonded in that unique way that only those who have survived the shipwreck of alcoholism can.

At the moment, we weren't allowed to shake hands or hold hands or in any way touch the inmates lest we try to pass contraband. So when the closing prayer rolled around, we apologized and told them they could join in any other way they liked. Then the three of us who had come in from the outside held hands with each other and formed a tiny circle.

"Our Father, who art in heaven," we began.

I'd expected the inmates to stand alone and apart from each other, as they often did, or at the most to form their own circle beside us. Instead, without exchanging a word, they silently, instinctively came together, joined hands, and like a fleet of guardian angels, formed their own larger circle with us in the middle.

Outside the circle were armed guards, bulletproof glass, metal doors, semi-automatic weapons, barbed wire, helicopters, guard dogs, security cameras. But the real security, the real power, lay inside.

"Lead us not into temptation," we prayed—we and the criminals—"but deliver us from evil."

Surrounded by cross-dressers, sex offenders, deviants, junkies, whores, and thieves, I've never felt so safe in my life.

JUNE 3, 2016

40

Sin Makes Guilt and Guilt Makes Fear, and Fear and Guilt Make More Sin

Michael Leach

> *I will heal their backsliding, and love them freely.*
>
> —Hosea 14:4–7

On the eve of my twelfth birthday, under the sign of Leo the Lion, and up on the roof of my uncle's garage, Roman Cracow taught me the facts of life.

A cold wind moved in from the lake, blowing westward away from home. A gentle voice called from a faraway porch, "Michael, your supper's ready."

"That's my mom," I said. "I gotta go."

Another voice bellowed from a nearby basement, "Roman, come and get it!"

"That's my old man," Roman said. "I gotta come and get it. Listen now, you don't tell nobody about them eight-pagers. You understand?"

I shook my head yes.

"Okay. You're cool. Go ahead."

I climbed carefully over the edge of the roof and shimmied down the rain gutter, thinking I should have slid through it instead. Roman hung to the edge of the rail and jumped. He didn't even hurt his feet. Then he grinned, gave me a wink, and waved goodbye.

I wandered down the alley in a daze. I bumped into a garbage can, tripped over a mattress, and mumbled to myself in front of a coalman. Later, when my mother looked me in the eyes, I knew that she knew that I knew. But I didn't think she knew that I knew that she knew. So I kept my mouth shut.

I had discovered the mystery of my own body, a discovery that became as frightening as it was exciting. It happened by accident at the end of a *Flash Gordon* chapter on WGN's *Saturday Morning Playhouse*. The Hawk Man, saliva dripping down his chin, wings flapping, cornered a flimsily clad Dale Arden. Dale breathed heavily, her two reasons for stardom heaving over her halter. The Hawk Man stretched out a hairy hand. Unconsciously, my hand moved too. Dale clutched her throat. Hawk Man leered. Dale screamed. The planet Mongo detonated.

I couldn't wait to shed my guilt. That afternoon I raced my Schwinn down Addison Street to St. Andrew's Church. Confessions began at 4 p.m. I sought out a ninety-year-old priest from Sicily who had hair in his ears. I entered his box. The shutter slid open. I confessed my shame and prayed he wouldn't probe. Thank God, he was pastoral. He asked me if took cold baths. I said no. He said take. He asked me if I slept with the window open. I said in the summer. He said winter, spring, and fall. He asked me if I ran around the block. I said only when somebody was chasing me. He said run.

Absolved, I crept out of the box, said ten Hail Marys, and pedaled home. That night I took a cold bath. Then I ran around the block. At night I slept with the window open. The next morning I woke up with a terrible cold. I had to stay in bed all day, daydreamed about Sandra Dee, and did the same bad thing again. The next Saturday I raced my Schwinn down Addison Street for afternoon confessions at St. Andrew's.

In eighth grade we had a day of retreat. The priest who gave it carried a huge cross in his sash like a sawed-off shotgun. He spoke about the dangers of the solitary sin. He didn't tell us that playing with ourselves could make us go crazy. Cracow told me that. But he did invite us to put our hands over a small fire. He scared the hell into us.

So, the next morning I raced my Schwinn down Addison Street for confessions before early morning mass. Then another sin and more guilt. Leading to more fear. Leading to more sin. *Ad nauseam*. Oh, the horror!

It wasn't until I was fifty and was frank with a couple of contemporaries that I learned I had been a normal Catholic boy.

I also learned that the only remedy to what most of us experience as sin is not guilt but forgiveness, not fear but gentle love, like that of a mother calling from a back porch, "Come home, your supper's ready."

Life is hard, for Roman Cracow too, and we all seek relief from the pain of being human, distractions from a low-grade fever of despair. We don't want to hurt anyone because we've been hurt, so our sins, if that's what they are, are mostly solitary: daydreaming that we're somebody we're not, touching ourselves to make sure we're alive, bragging so others will like us, being ungrateful when we have everything we need, envying others who have a little bit more, consuming mass quantities of wine or Cheese Puffs, porn or TV, or all four at once. Many of us feel tremendous guilt over our pathetic habits, especially those below the belt. We fear that God will punish us, and the only thing we know to do is escape some more. We even stop praying or spiritual reading because we think, what's the point? we're bad. Guilt makes fear, and fear makes sin, and sin makes guilt, and guilt makes us afraid and so we sin again to escape more guilt and fear. It is the human condition, the original sin of thinking that God will abandon us and not let us back Home because we once ate a piece of rotten fruit. God says instead, "Come Home! Who told you that you were naked? I have a banquet prepared for you. In truth, you never left me."

As long as we put value on guilt and fear, we will be like the snake that eats its own tail. Healing from sin begins when we forgive ourselves and have compassion for others even as we backslide. God always forgives because

Love never blames. So never stop saying your prayers or reading spiritual books. Your mother has a higher opinion of you than you do.

MAY 22, 2015

✧ SIGHTING ✧

There is a crack in everything. That's how the light gets in.

—LEONARD COHEN

41

Love Revealed in Brokenness

Heidi Russell

"Children born to another woman call me 'Mom.' The magnitude of that tragedy and the depth of that privilege are not lost on me."

I read this quote by Jody Landers on a lot of Facebook pages of other foster and adoptive moms, and I have posted it on my own. Being a parent is always a privilege, but when you become a parent through foster care and adoption, the emotional mix has a different level of complexity.

My children have two mothers, both of whom love them. One thing that I have learned from the foster care world is that even parents facing insurmountable challenges in learning how to parent a child love their children. The first time I saw my son's other mother was in a courtroom in Milwaukee. I had to hold my breath to keep from crying when she walked in, because I looked at her face and saw my son. I was overwhelmed with love in that moment, and my heart was ready to burst with gratitude to her for giving my son the gift of life. Up to that moment she had been a name on a piece of paper, and it is all too easy and human, and yes, sinful, to demonize a name on paper. Standing face to face with my son's mother and realizing that both of us loved the same child, I became connected to her for life in a way I could not have imagined. In that moment of connection my own well being and happiness became tied up with hers. I could only want what was best for her, even as the thought of that leading to my never seeing my son again terrified me. There are no prayers at that time, beyond the prayer for the presence of God as Love, because there is no ending where everyone will be happy. Hearts would be broken. I could not even pray, "Thy will be done," because there was no ending that seemed like it could possibly be God's will.

In a foster-parent class one of our teachers broached the topic of getting attached to a child placed with you through foster care. She said, "If you think you can be a foster parent and not get attached, then you should not be a foster parent. These kids deserve to have parents who are attached." When people find out that you are a foster parent, one of the most common things you hear is: "Oh, I couldn't do that. I would get too attached" or "I would be too afraid of losing the child." Hence one of the other oft-posted foster parent quotes is: "I am not afraid to grieve. I am afraid of what would happen to these children, if no one took the risk to love them." For me, it would be a lie to say that I wasn't or am not afraid to grieve, but the love casts out the fear. At a point in time when I thought my son's case was moving toward reunification, I was terrified, but I remember thinking that I would not take back one second of the time I had with him to avoid the heartbreak. Such is the gift of love. Love casts out fear. While I couldn't imagine living without him, even more, I couldn't imagine never having had the privilege to love him. The grief and loss of this journey, however, is multifaceted.

The day I sat in a courtroom and listened to my son's other mother cry as her lawyer told the judge that she wanted to voluntarily terminate her parental rights was the day I learned what self-sacrificial love means. Tears ran down my own face, and afterward, I sobbed in my car—for her loss, for my son's loss, for the brokenness of the world that brought us all to this point, for the gift of forgiveness. My son's first mother taught me what it means to lay down your life for those you love. My understanding of the love poured out in the crucifixion, a love that forgives and gives life to others at one's own expense, deepened in watching her pour out her love for her son in a way that denied her own life and being. I pray that resurrection comes from her selfless gift, but the world is not a Hallmark movie. Reality is much more . . . well . . . real. The challenges that led her to the point where she stood in that courtroom that day did not disappear from her life. The brokenness of our world and the cycles of poverty, racism, incarceration, addiction, mental illness, abuse, and so forth that bring so many people in our society to their knees have not been overcome. And so, while we are a resurrection people, we are challenged not to gloss over what led to the crucifixion of Love in our midst, that injustice and oppression that still crucifies love in our midst today. That Love revealed in crucifixion must challenge me to push past my own comfort and privilege to confront the systemic injustice that has led both to the greatest joy of my life in the presence of my son and the deepest tragedy of my son's life in the loss of his mother. Another woman's child calls me Mom. The magnitude of that tragedy and depth of that privilege must not be lost on me.

JANUARY 30, 2017

42

Brokenness Lets Us See Where True Beauty Lies

Mary DeTurris Poust

If you look around my office prayer space or on my bedroom dresser, you'll notice one constant: broken conch and whelk shells everywhere. Small and blue-gray, large and sun bleached, twisting, turning, spiraling in that gorgeous and mysterious way that seashells do. Although I have one perfect channeled whelk shell that I purchased in Cape May, New Jersey, years ago, my prized possessions are broken shells of every shape and size because, as far as I'm concerned, they are far more beautiful than the ones that are perfectly intact and so lovely on the outside.

I love the way the brokenness lets you see inside, where the true beauty lies. There you discover the magnificent soft turns and intricate work of the Creator typically hidden by the outer shell, details so beautiful you would gasp if a sculptor had crafted them out of marble. Yet there they are, lying on the sand, trampled underfoot, washed ashore and pulled back out by the next tide along with tangled seaweed and discarded cigarette butts, or, every so often, tucked into the pocket of a hoodie by someone hoping for a sacred souvenir, a reminder that even some of God's most beautiful creations are cracked and dulled and hobbled by the pounding surf of daily life.

I think I'm so taken with these shell fragments because they remind me of people, broken but beautiful. Even the people who look physically perfect on the outside harbor an intricate beauty and brokenness somewhere on the inside. It's just a factor of our humanity. We don't get through this life whole and intact; we are meant to be broken open, to expose and embrace our inner beauty.

But that's not easy. I don't know about you, but I have a hard time looking at myself with the same gentle eyes I use to look at my collection of scarred and shattered shells. I understand in theory that "I am wonderfully made," as Psalm 139 tells us, but translating that into an attitude that guides my daily life is a challenge. In my mind's eye I see only the imperfections in the creation that I am. I would be wonderfully made, if only . . . *(fill in the blank)*. I may believe God has an unconditional love for everyone else on the planet, but believing that about myself is, well, unbelievable.

I struggled with that concept throughout the writing of my book *Cravings: A Catholic Wrestles with Food, Self-Image, and God,* where I explored the ways we allow our hunger for wholeness to fuel unhealthy urges—whether for food, alcohol, shopping, gossip, sex, gambling, or any other empty "vice"—that only pull us farther and farther away from understanding our true self and recognizing our beloved-ness in God's eyes.

"Our brokenness is truly ours. Nobody else's. Our bro-kenness is as unique as our chosenness and our blessedness," writes Henri Nouwen in *Life of the Beloved*. "As fearsome as it may sound, as the Beloved ones, we are called to claim our unique brokenness, just as we have to claim our unique chosenness and our unique blessedness."

Can we begin to see our brokenness as a blessing rather than a curse, a beauty mark rather than a scar? It can hap-pen only when we fully place ourselves in God's hands and accept once and for all that we are indeed wonderfully made, even with—or maybe because of—our flaws and weaknesses, our wrinkles and quirks, our sins and struggles. God doesn't love us only after we are "fixed." God loves us into being and loves us through our imperfections, pa-tiently waiting for us to climb on board and revel in that gift. Unfortunately we are too often caught up in the mi-rage of wholeness, the mistaken belief that a perfect outer shell will make us more lovable.

We are so busy spinning our wheels in an effort to become shiny and unblemished to the outside world that we miss the still, small voice urging us on from the inside, the Spirit beckoning us to stop spinning, stop judging, and rest in the arms of God exactly as we are at this moment, knowing we are loved perfectly despite our imperfections.

We are all shattered in one way or another. We are all incomplete, missing pieces here and there. But we are all beautiful. In fact, we are more beautiful because of our imperfections. Who wants polished perfection that belies the truth of what's inside when you can have the raw power of beauty that's broken because it has lived and loved and lost and carried on in spite of it all? Be broken and be beautiful.

FEBRUARY 14, 2014

43

Jesus, Wash My Ugly, Dirty, Swollen Feet, Wash All of Me

Sue Stanton

Watching my daughter graduate as a white minority student from nursing school, I wonder just how many varied kinds of feet she will wash in her new career as a nurse. Toughened up by miles of being walked on, our feet are witness to those barefoot times we step into our baby's room to check on him or her, the shoes we shove them into praying they won't be too tight, the sandals, the pedicures, the lotions, the wool socks we knit for them. It is our feet that show our age, our history, even our ancestry, in ways nothing else can.

I remember thinking of Mary, mother of Jesus, as I stood, glimpsing a pair of sandaled feet across from me in the Palestinian line at a checkpoint on the West Bank. The young mother has a four-year-old son with her, who tugs at her hands and long black skirt.

Her feet are thick with calluses, her sandals durable but worn down in the back where she has had to carry large heavy bundles such as a child in her arms.

Those powerful words of Jesus ring in my ears; "Whoever does not receive you, nor heed your words, as you go out of that house or that city, shake the dust off your feet."

Yet shaking dust off is easier said than done, and I think of how many times during visits Jesus and Mary had to wash their feet upon entering any home.

The idea of washing feet is a highly charged one throughout history. Because it was considered the filthiest part of the body (as well as a metaphor for other body parts), it was the most reviled job of all.

Yet Jesus teaches: If I do not wash you and your ugly, dirty, barnacle-looking swollen feet, you have no part with me.

Can we really accept such a radical concept of service? Accept the entire human body as an altar for service with, to, and for others?

This is the time of year when thousands of young people graduate and embark on careers in service to others. These others have bodies too—they are the altars of God, the high places that will be practiced upon.

But have we as a society encouraged such service, or have we become so tied up with the idea of financial outcomes, winners and losers, that service to others, our communities, our world has become merely a naive concept filled?

We already live in a present where there is a decrease in scientists, physicians, teachers, nurses, postal workers, policemen, farm workers, and farm owners. These positions are becoming ever more difficult to fill for any number of reasons, as the need grows for quality not quantity.

Have our children and grandchildren been given examples of public figures who command respect and who will inspire them to follow, dare we say, noble goals?

Have we raised those minority voices of struggle and achievement, many times doing so through noble goals, to the forefront of our awareness where they can actually encourage us?

Standing in line with a Palestinian woman I saw my own future as a minority. Here in this world where minorities lack rights, I realized that one day I'll lack them too. I will be elderly, God willing, and be placed in a category. Our bodies will continue to define us, as well as stifle the future, as long as human beings judge one another on appearance, actions, and the millions of thoughts that come out of them totally unfiltered.

Mercifully, St. Peter gives us a model answer when he says to Jesus, If you insist on washing my feet, then wash all of me as well.

It is a commencement speech, however brief, as he pledges his entire self to the service of the Lord. The entire body, not just the clean parts but the calloused parts, the stupid and foolish parts, the parts that will make mistakes and the parts that will reject others and act disgusting, all are pledged to service.

How timely that Pope Francis has placed us in this Year of Mercy when our national electoral process is here. We can see and experience actions to others and for others as we journey on foot in the communal life and well being of the church.

44

Embarrassment Is a Doorway to Grace

Michael Leach

> *All human nature vigorously resists grace because grace changes us and the change is painful.*
>
> —FLANNERY O'CONNOR,
> *THE HABIT OF BEING*

Many years ago the painful truth that I was more interested in being "a nice guy," a people pleaser, than the kind individual I thought I was came to my attention and was killing me. I didn't want to face it. I didn't want anyone to know it. I was at a crossroad of grace and could either stay asleep or awake from a bad dream.

I was with Vickie, sitting in our car in front of Baskin-Robbins. I had to tell her. My thoughts poured out like soft-serve ice cream. I was embarrassed. Though I knew better, I feared she would think less of me. *Me*, a phony? What could be worse?

"I know," she said. "It's all right."

"I've spent my whole life trying to get people to like me," I confessed.

"I know," she said. "It was the only way you knew to get through life. It's all right."

I talked, Vickie listened, her few words were the right words. The pressure in me started to release like someone else's bad breath coming out of a punctured balloon. "I've really gotten good at it, haven't I?" I said.

"Nobody does it better!"

We both laughed. And my laughter turned to tears. The kind that heals.

The courage to be embarrassed is a doorway to grace.

And it only hurts for a moment.

"Sweetheart," she assured me, "you are the kindest man I've ever known. Nobody's perfect."

I knew then, in front of Baskin-Robbins, what Julian of Norwich knew eight centuries ago when she thought she was facing death: "All shall be well, and all shall be well, and all manner of thing shall be well."

Peter must have had a day like that when he jumped off the boat to walk on water as Jesus did, only to sink like a crozier. How embarrassing to realize you're a fool. How healing to be told, "Peter, upon your imperfect character I will build my church!"

It takes the grace of embarrassment to face our foolishness and then accept the assurance that despite our lack of understanding, in Jesus's eyes we are perfect even as our heavenly Father is perfect. Dr. Thomas Hora, a psychiatrist and spiritual teacher, used to say that we would rather confess to murder than to being ignorant. Admitting that we don't know something, especially a thought that hides in our hearts, is too embarrassing. But he reminded his students, "The heat of embarrassment is the consuming fire of 'hell' in which the ego is annihilated." A Zen Master earlier counseled: "Erase yourself, utterly." Jesus taught, "Those who find their life will lose it." We cannot do this without risking embarrassment.

Embarrassment is not the same as being ashamed. Shame is the handmaiden of guilt. It says, "Look at me! I'm awful!" Embarrassment is the companion of truth. It says, "Look away from me! I'm weak." The Bible comforts the embarrassed: "Who is weak, and I am not weak? Who is made to stumble, and I am not inflamed?" (2 Cor 11:29). Guilt is a form of bragging. Embarrassment is a sign of humility. It grounds us, invites God to make us whole.

In the movie *We Bought a Zoo*, Matt Damon encourages his teenage son, who is afraid to tell the girl he loves what he feels: "You know, sometimes all you need is twenty seconds of insane courage. Just literally twenty seconds of just embarrassing bravery. And I promise you, something great will come of it." Whenever we are willing to be embarrassed, as I was with Vickie at Baskin-Robbins, as Peter was all the time with Jesus, as many Catholics are in the confessional, truth reveals itself and it doesn't really hurt, it sets us free.

My journey to Baskin-Robbins began when I was about nineteen and read a huge hardcover book with a shiny blue jacket called *Kindness*. I wish I still had it. It was then that I knew: kindness was the value that I valued more than any other. I had always given away my comic books as a kid and never wanted anything in return, often to the dismay of my mother. I learned that good things come from kindness, and that other values follow in joyful step like the Trapp kids prancing after Julie Andrews. I'd also learn, through experiences of distress more than through wisdom, that the desire to be unconditionally kind and helpful has a shadow side: an insatiable hunger for love masked as approval, applause, or affection. Manipulation, even unintended, lurks in the moonlight of our consciousness like the Wolfman. Once that discovery of darkness blew through the hole in my heart and into my awareness, I was able to tell Vickie, like the boy with his twenty seconds of embarrassing bravery, what I had been discerning about a lifetime of mixed motives. I lost my life that day. I found the life that was already there. And our hot-fudge sundaes never tasted so good.

SEPTEMBER 11, 2012

✧ SIGHTING ✧

Peter Asks Jesus a Question

Then Peter asked, "Lord, how often should I forgive some-
one who sins against me? Seven times?"

"No, not seven times," Jesus answered, "but seventy
times seven."

—MATTHEW 18:21–22

45

What Does Everyday Mercy Look Like?

Vinita Hampton Wright

The publishing company I work for recently released the US edition of *The Church of Mercy* by Pope Francis. This book conveys the pope's vision for a church that could become a healing force in the world simply by communicating and demonstrating the mercy of God.

Little wonder that the word "mercy" beat in my heart for weeks and along with it the question: What does mercy look like? How might I become a person of mercy? In the Christian vocabulary, mercy is a forgiving response to wrongdoing; it is God's countermove to our sin. Having lived intentionally as a Christian for more than forty years, I have avoided the easily labeled sins, acts that would require my arrest or resignation. Yet, I am a persistent sinner. When a reporter asked Pope Francis, "Who are you?" he answered, "I am a sinner"—I knew, at least I'm in good company. Our pope has named, however, the grand antidote to sin, which is mercy.

As I move through this day, how will I live mercifully? What words and actions will express to others around me the mercy Pope Francis is talking about? In a given day I do ordinary things, and I traverse a fairly unexciting landscape. My mercy will not show up in grand gestures, and most of the time mercy reveals itself in fleeting moments.

For example, mercy gives you his seat on the bus, acting as if he was about to get up anyway rather than making you feel that he is doing you a favor. Mercy does not let out that sigh—you know the one—the wordless disapproval toward the person in the check-out line ahead of you whose card didn't swipe or who can't find her coupons, or whose toddler is having a meltdown. Mercy offers quiet sympathy and does not convey with her body language that this hold-up is ruining her day. Sometimes mercy chooses not to send back the food that isn't just right, simply because the waitress looks overwhelmed.

When mercy has been wronged, the offended one does not make it difficult for the offender to apologize or ask forgiveness. In fact, mercy does not wait for the other's action but forgives so quickly that the person needing forgiveness is freer to ask for it. Likewise, at work, home, or in the classroom, mercy creates an atmosphere in which a person feels safe enough to admit his mistake or ask a question. And if mercy must correct someone, it pains her to do it, and she does so gently, without vindictive relish.

Mercy makes a habit of giving others the benefit of the doubt. Mercy is not in the habit of sending deadly glares at people who are annoying. Mercy gives charitably, knowing that eventually someone will take advantage of his generosity. Mercy welcomes you, fully aware that this act may disrupt her own plans.

Mercy relinquishes control when doing so allows another person to grow and learn. Mercy makes it his business to help others succeed. Mercy clears the way for others, so that they can walk on an even path, no matter how halting their steps or injured their souls.

In all these situations, mercy treats power as a sacred trust. I can be merciful because I have some sort of power, the means to affect another's life, if only for a moment. I act mercifully when I use my power to do kindness in this world.

I was at a conference recently, and it was interesting to observe how the well-known, powerful people wore their power, how they responded to others' admiration, how they spoke to those who were not so well known or admired. Some used their power to make room for others and invite their voices; others used their power to dominate the space and the conversation. In my own work I have achieved a certain level of expertise and others' respect. When I sit in a room with colleagues, they feel the weight of my opinions. With a sentence or a glance I can crush or I can encourage. I can open up the conversation or shut it down.

Most of my sins involve failure at mercy. Whether through my unhopeful opinion of someone, my silent sentences that criticize him, my words grinding away in the privacy of a moving car, my neglect to help, or my refusal to notice when help is needed—each failure of mercy denies the community a bit of healing that might have happened.

Thus, mercy has become my new sin detector, a personal barometer. *Am I showing mercy?* makes for self-assessment that is simple, direct, and difficult to misinterpret.

AUGUST 29, 2014

46

What Ever Happened to Lil' Miss Hegel?

Michael Leach

> *He departed from our sight so we might*
> *return to our heart and find him there.*
> *For he departed, and behold, he is here.*
> —St. Augustine

Here it is, Eastertime, and I'm thinking of Lil' Miss Hegel, whom I last saw in 1958. She was a little old lady who used to visit my great grandmother's house across the street from Hamilton School. Grandma Gengenbach (pronounced GAY-Ghen-Bach) didn't talk much, didn't care to. She liked company about as much as Beethoven did.

It was maybe 1950 and I was nine when I first met Lil' Miss Hegel, a wisp of a woman no taller than I, who dressed in black and wore a hat with a veil. Her eyes were kindly squints, with an occasional tear squeezing out of one of them which she dabbed with a hankie. She sat in the upholstered chair and held her cup of tea and saucer like a lady. Grandma Gengenbach slumped in the overstuffed easy chair across from her and tapped her fingers on the arm rest. They talked in German so I didn't understand why my great grandmother seemed especially impatient.

I sat on the blue sofa with my beloved Gramma Lou (her daughter, my dad's mother) for a while and then she and I went out to the front porch and rocked on the swing. "Gramma," I asked, "why doesn't Grandma Gengenbach like Lil' Miss Hegel?"

"She likes her. She just gets annoyed sometimes like she does with all of us."

"Why? Miss Hegel is quiet."

"Miss Hegel is very old and sometimes says the same things over and over again."

Months later I'm sitting on the sofa with Gramma Lou, reading a comic book, and the doorbell rings. "Hide!" Gramma Lou says.

"Don't answer it!" Grandma Gengenbach tells me.

By then I'm opening the door. There is Lil' Miss Hegel, a smile on her face, a small carton from Dinkel's Bakery in her hands, stockings crawling down her legs. She has walked a long way.

Gramma Lou says hello and goes to the kitchen to make some tea. Grandma Gengenbach gives me a look.

"You must be Betty Lou's grandson," Miss Hegel tweets. "I bet you go to school across the street."

"No, ma'am, I go to St. Andrew's."

"I bet you like cookies though. Come here, dear, take one."

I take out a cinnamon cookie.

"Have another," she says.

She starts to speak to Grandma Gengenbach in German. I try to follow and every time I hear the same sounds from Miss Hegel I see my great grandmother gripping the arms of her chair. I want to go across the street to the playground but stay. Miss Hegel smiles at me. "You must be Betty Lou's grandson," she says. "I bet you like cookies."

"He's had enough," Grandma Gengenbach says and pulls herself up from her chair.

The next time I see Lil' Miss Hegel is a couple of years later. I'm walking up a side street on my way to Gramma Lou's when I spot her on the corner of Ashland Avenue, a block away from the house.

"Hi, Miss Hegel, are you lost?"

She looks at me like she never saw me before. She is trembling. She smells of urine.

"Would you like me to take you to my grandmother's house?"

I hold her hand. It's soft and cold, like a scared bird. As we climb the steps to the porch I sense the scurrying inside. The door is unlocked. I open it and soon we're all seated and Lil' Miss Hegel smiles at me and asks, "Are you Betty Lou's son?"

Which brings us to spring 1958 and the last time I ever saw her.

I'm seventeen and driving my first car, a 1946 grey Pontiac, up Addison Street on the way to St. Andrew's

Gym for a basketball game. Again, just up ahead, near Ashland, stands a little old lady in a black dress wearing a black hat with a veil, her head darting this way and that. I can't be late for the game. Grandma Gengenbach is gone. I slow down to put Lil' Miss Hegel in the car so I can quickly get her to wherever she lives. But I don't know where she lives and she won't be able to tell me so instead of stopping I keep on driving. I rush through a yellow light at Ashland and pull up in front of the gym. I keep the motor running.

Damn!

I'll find a cop. I speed up to Lincoln Avenue and turn left all the way to Belmont and back again. Not a cop in sight.

I go back to put Miss Hegel in the car. I'll think of something then.

But she isn't there.

She isn't a block behind, a block to the left, a block to the right. She isn't anywhere.

I go to the game, a hole in my heart the size of an empty net.

And now it's Eastertime 2016 and I am taking care of my wife, Vickie, who has Alzheimer's and who makes sounds over and over that don't make sense, and I am thinking of Lil' Miss Hegel and wondering what ever happened to her.

Please pray for us, Miss Hegel.

Forgive me for passing you by at Addison and Ashland so many years ago.

Help me to be good and to understand the meaning of your presence in my life.

Did you come to me then to prepare me for what was to come half a century later?

Do you come to me now at Eastertime to remind me what is important is not that Jesus rose from the dead but *why*. I've been learning my whole life that he died to save us and rose to demonstrate that everything he taught us was true.

And what he taught us most was to love the weakest amongst us.

Thank you, Miss Hegel, for inspiring me to be faithful to my promise to Vickie to have and to hold, to love and to cherish, in sickness as well as in health.

Like the Lord himself you departed from my sight so I might return again to my heart and this time find you there. For you departed and behold, like E.T.—like Christ himself—you are *right here*.

MARCH 25, 2016

47

A Leper's Dance of Gratitude

Maureen Sinnott

During my nine trips to Tanzania I have met many women and men with leprosy, but none touched my heart as deeply as Mama Rosalia. She is not only an outcast from Tanzanian society but also an outcast from her leper village in Katoke. Why? Because someone spread false rumors about her being a witch doctor and the other lepers began to fear and shun her. In truth, she is just a lonely, vulnerable, homeless widow sleeping under the stars, sadly abandoned even by her own children. Her fingers and toes are severely deformed and she walks in pain due to open wounds on her feet.

One of our Franciscan Sisters of Penance and Christian Charity, Sr. Liesbeth Runes from Indonesia, befriended her some years ago, and their relationship has developed into what could only be described as "Sacred Sisterhood." Liesbeth even began to dream the impossible dream of building Mama Rosalia a little house of her own. This year that dream actually came true when Liesbeth celebrated her Fortieth Jubilee and could share her monetary gifts with

Mama. Last month in the mid-day African heat she was able as Aspirant Directress to not only teach our aspirants Franciscan spirituality but also how to incarnate it in service to others by building a small house for Mama Rosalia.

The Aspirant convent borders the leper village, so every day between prayers and study Sr. Liesbeth led sixteen of our Aspirants to fetch water, carry the heavy buckets on their heads, and walk to where the house was to be built. They then dug a hole and kneaded the water with their bare feet into the dirt to make "cement." With their bare hands they took the "cement" and threw it into the holes between the small homemade bricks that were the walls of the house. When the house was almost completed (within a week's time) and the sun was setting it was too late for the two men who were helping to assemble the roof or to make the door. Nevertheless, door or no door, Mama Rosalia insisted on sleeping inside on the bare earth to guard her little home from dangerous robbers in the area. We watched her carry all her possessions in a small sack and reverently place them in her new space. We noticed a small pot of beans cooking on an open fire and asked what she had eaten so far that day. Her simple reply: "Nothing. I eat one meal a day of beans."

The next day Sr. Liesbeth led us in a prayerful blessing of the house with holy water asking God to protect Mama Rosalia from all harm. At the end of the blessing, Mama, with a smile that radiated like sunshine, struggled with her deformed and painful feet to do a little dance of gratitude. It was a moment of Thanksgiving I will remember all the days of my life. I asked myself: If I had leprosy and lost mobility of my fingers and toes, lost my husband and children, looked forward to only one meal a day of beans, relieved myself in the bushes, carried water on my head from a distance for cooking and bathing, was treated as an outcast from society, was shunned by my leper community, and lost my reputation due to false rumors, would I still be able to smile and do a dance to a silent tune of gratitude?

NOVEMBER 23, 2012

48

A Grateful Heart Is the Grace of a Second Chance

John, a member of Al-Anon

> *Piglet noticed that even though he had*
> *a very small heart, it could hold a rather*
> *large amount of gratitude.*
> —A. A. MILNE, *WINNIE-THE-POOH*

Ten years after the crisis that sent my brother to alcoholism treatment and me to Al-Anon, I rarely miss my weekly Al-Anon Steps and Traditions group meeting. Come Thanksgiving my brother will mark ten years of sobriety, and I ten years of learning, over and over again, that my heart has more room for gratitude than I ever knew.

Gratitude never worked in me the way I learned it was supposed to growing up. What I read about virtue just

---

John is the pseudonym of an American theologian. AA and Al-Anon ask their members to remain anonymous in public, saying in the "12th tradition" that "anonymity is the spiritual foundation of all our traditions, ever reminding us to place principles above personalities."

made me nervous: if we are "brought up in fine habits," Aristotle wrote, our virtues will take deep root and thenceforth shine forth as "firm and constant." If only we choose our parents well (and are born the right race and gender) we will be among the "great-souled men" showing others how to live.

Alas, both my soul and heart have always felt rather small, like Piglet's. My gratitude has not been firm and constant. But a deep sense of gratitude has come over me from time to time these last ten years—more often than not when I've been sitting in an Al-Anon meeting.

I remember distinctly my second ever Al-Anon meeting, at the alcoholism treatment center shortly after my brother entered treatment there. A handful of his siblings, his wife, and their not yet two-year-old daughter all joined my brother for lunch and the meeting. The leader read to us that "Al-Anon is a fellowship of relatives and friends of alcoholics who share their experience, strength, and hope in order to solve their common problems."

My brother's head was down and I fidgeted in my chair. Then we heard the voice of the woman leader calling to my niece who was toddling around in the circle of gathered people. My niece walked over to the woman, who took her in her arms and announced to the group, "How lucky this girl is—she's going to grow up in a house of recovery!" My heart calmed and my brain stopped racing. That, in my experience, is how gratitude feels when it comes—a slowing, resting, and opening. This bodily sense did not remain long that day, or any other day, but it has its effects. I went out from the treatment center a little less anxious, less shut down, with my heart a little more open.

Later I experienced this almost every time a man named Jim spoke at my regular Al-Anon meeting. He had been to hell and back—through his own alcoholism and his wife's, through a depression that hospitalized him repeatedly for electro-convulsive therapy. The crises had ended some years before I met Jim. Yet there he was each week beginning his sharing at meetings with this phrase: "an attitude of gratitude; and gratitude is my attitude."

I hadn't noticed before meeting him in Al-Anon that Jim was an usher in the church I attended. His smile as I walked into church those days opened the eye of my soul, an experience of grace if I have ever had one. He's dead now six or seven years, but I can still hear his voice and see his smile. And as I do, my heart opens again.

There are others at that Al-Anon meeting: Richard, whose now ex-wife became so lost in alcohol she had become a danger not only to herself and Richard, but also to their only daughter. Richard's health is not great, and he works two jobs to support himself and his daughter, now in college. He begins his sharing at meetings with the same line every time: "I'm Richard; I'm still here and I'm grateful."

And there is Sylvia, who comes from a religious home—she's a "preacher's kid"—in which there was abuse of all kinds (physical, emotional, sexual), all fueled by alcoholism. She lost a sibling to suicide a few years ago, and she often gets anxious, but I watch at meetings and sometimes see the rest and openness of gratitude come over her. She says Al-Anon is why she is alive.

I sat down with my brother the other day to ask him about gratitude, and here's what he said:

> When I was first in recovery, I tried to learn to be grateful. I'd think, "I forgot to pray. . . . I have to work more at being grateful." But a few years ago it came to me that I just don't like who I am when I am not grateful—making my case against people and nursing resentments. When I am not grateful I fall into what AA calls "self-inflicted misery." Gratitude is not about finding a litany of things to be grateful for anymore. It's just my best option for living.

Isn't it interesting that none of the people I've met over the last ten years in Al-Anon came to their gratitude the way Aristotle said it should happen? That gets me thinking: maybe *no one* fits Aristotle's version of the moral life, and maybe Al-Anon is calming me enough to give up on trying. Maybe University of Notre Dame moral theologian Jean Porter was talking about *all of us* when she wrote that those "whose virtues are due to infusion (of God's grace), may well experience more distress in leading the good life, and exhibit more actual imperfection, than the person who possesses the acquired virtues"—that is, Aristotle's virtues.

Maybe no one ever "acquired" gratitude by being well brought up. Maybe we have all been graced into it as a second chance.

Such has been my experience of gratitude in Al-Anon—a slowing that comes upon me from time to time and allows me to open my small heart and live from a more loving posture than I knew was possible. With a little luck (or grace) I will be there in Al-Anon for ten more years and beyond, seeing where this gratitude can take me.

NOVEMBER 22, 2013

49

Bishop Morrie Has a Remembrance of Things Past

Michael Leach

Every October a dozen of my classmates—St. Mary of the Lake Seminary, 1966—gather again to give ourselves a two-day retreat. Nine of us left the priesthood a long time ago to marry. One of the stalwarts who remained is Morrie, now the bishop of Paris, Kansas. Morrie and I are ambling around the lake as we did many times in the '60s, watching squirrels jump from branch to branch and leaves tremble yellow and gold.

"Remember, Morrie, when you and me and Ed and Charlie played soldiers in the woods?"

"Yeah, Ed used to bury himself under a ton of leaves like Rambo. He didn't show up for supper one night and we had to get a posse and search for him."

"I can't remember. Did we find him?"

"No, . . . We only had an hour free time before we had to go back to our rooms. Remember how the smokers would smoke as many cigarettes as they could because you could only smoke after meals? The rec room looked like Los Alamos."

"And if you walked around the lake with the same guy too often Fr. Fitzgerald would warn you about having a particular friendship. It wasn't till I was forty that I figured out what he was talking about."

"Yeah," Morrie says. "I thought a particular friendship meant you couldn't have a best friend. A priest was supposed to be like the Lone Ranger or the Cure of Ars who was a friend to those who have no friend and a member of all families but a member of none."

"You're thinking of Boston Blackie."

We walk in silence and let memories run through our minds like deer in an enchanted forest. Then Morrie speaks, in a softer tone: "Remember—it was maybe fifty years ago—we had ten years in, only two to go—Malachy Foley called you and me into his rector's office and said we couldn't be priests in Chicago because our parents were divorced."

"I'll never forget it," I say. "I was called in before you. He said it would cause scandal to the faithful. I told him that in the minor seminary Msgr. Howard told me about the rule and that it was wrong but I shouldn't worry because when I got ordained it would all be different."

"What did Mal tell you?"

"'Son,' he said, 'Msgr. Howard is dead.'"

"I was so unhappy," Morrie remembers. "I didn't want to be a priest some place where I didn't know the streets."

"I was crushed, but I still wanted to be a priest and make people happy. When I got home that Christmas, I checked in with my pastor. I asked him where he thought I should apply. He was furious. He got on the phone and called up Mal and yelled: 'Don't you ever say anything like that to this boy again and don't you *dare* say anything bad about his mother, you hear me? She's a good Catholic and her son will be a priest in Chicago!'"

"And you were."

"And you weren't."

"My pastor wasn't Bishop Sheil."

"I feel bad."

"Don't. I can see Paris from my back porch."

We stop at the little red-bricked bridge with black lanterns at the halfway point and watch the water ripple toward the distant chapel atop a hill. "Morrie, why did you choose to go to Paris, Kansas?"

"Well, to tell you the truth, it had a lot to do with that commie newspaper you write for, the *National Catholic Enquirer.*"

"Reporter."

"I know. In 1964—fifty years ago maybe to this day—that's when it began. They had these inspiring stories about parishes doing wonderful things during the Vatican Council. The newspaper was in Kansas City, so I said, 'I'll be a priest in Kansas.'"

"Kansas City is in Missouri."

"Still is. And I'm the pastor of Paris. Haven't missed an issue of *NCR* since."

"You know," I say, "looking back on that experience with Mal makes me think about what Steve Hazard was talking about this morning."

"His grandchildren?"

"No, Mandela."

"You guys are always talking about your grandchildren. Nobody cares."

"He quoted Nelson Mandela when he was leaving prison. Mandela wrote something like, 'As I walked toward the gate that would give me freedom, I knew if I didn't leave my bitterness behind I'd still be in prison.' I've forgiven Msgr. Foley many times over the years for a lot of things but still feel a burn in my gut when this one comes back up."

Morrie turns to me. "It's time to stop forgiving him. You've done your seventy times seven. It's time to forgive yourself for not feeling it. Nobody's perfect."

A cool October breeze whips up and blows a whirl of leaves across our ankles. I look past Morrie into the woods and just look. "I see the forest," I tell him.

"I see Ed. He looks like Bigfoot. Let's move on."

OCTOBER 25, 2014

✦ SIGHTING ✦

An Adulteress Dodges a Stone

Now early in the morning he came again into the temple, and all the people came to him; and he sat down and taught them. Then the scribes and Pharisees brought to him a woman caught in adultery. And when they had set her in the midst, they said to him, "Teacher, this woman was caught in adultery, in the very act. Now Moses, in the law, commanded] us that such should be stoned. But what do You say?" This they said, testing him, that they might have something of which to accuse him. But Jesus stooped down and wrote on the ground with his finger, as though he did not hear.

So when they continued asking him, he raised himself up and said to them, "He who is without sin among you, let him throw a stone at her first." And again he stooped down and wrote on the ground. Then those who heard, being convicted by their conscience, went out one by one, beginning with the oldest even to the last. And Jesus was left alone, and the woman standing in the midst. When Jesus had raised himself up and saw no one but the woman, he said to her, "Woman, where are those accusers of yours? Has no one condemned you?"

She said, "No one, Lord."

And Jesus said to her, "Neither do I condemn you; go and sin no more."

—JOHN 8:2–11

50

A Message on Mortality from an American in Paris

Patrick Jephson

Usually I'm a pretty prompt unpacker. But for some reason I let the Paris suitcase I brought back home sit unopened for almost a week before, with a strange reluctance, I made myself unzip the lid and look inside. The familiar contents were a little creased and rumpled but otherwise unchanged since I had happily stowed them in the Samsonite ten days ago, already anticipating the prospect of the flight to France and the conference at which I was guest speaker.

Why the reluctance? Because now all that belonged to another world—the one that ended on Friday November 13, 2015. Neither the suitcase nor I stopped a terrorist bullet; the hotel room we shared hadn't been rocked by exploding suicide vests or the street spattered with blood and worse. But we were there in Paris on that night; and the corner of my brain that has time to think about eternity is asking why.

Back in suburban Washington DC, I watched the TV news like everybody else as the ISIS attacks and their gory aftermath were reported and repeatedly picked over as if sheer volume of airtime could explain immeasurables like good and evil. And as I eventually started unpacking, unconsciously labeling each item as worn *Before Friday* or *After Friday*, part of me was gnawing at questions of chance and free will that CNN couldn't be expected to answer.

The suitcase—faithful companion on scores of journeys to wilder spots than France—held no answers. That is, until only one thing remained: a French flag, made of thick shiny paper and mounted on a plastic stick. The stick was now bent and the paper crumpled, but as I held the flimsy red, white, and blue scrap a pattern slowly formed in my mind.

I had arrived in Paris on November 11 and took the bus to the Champs Elysees where a thin line of spectators was standing on the pavement, looking downhill toward the Place de la Concorde. I had forgotten it was Armistice Day, and the time was nearing 11 a.m., the moment of most solemn remembrance. I could hear the drums of an approaching military band and soon the cavalry of the Garde Republicainne came gloriously into view, rank after rank of snorting chargers and their splendidly uniformed riders, faces implacable under plumed helmets, sabers drawn. Suddenly you could guess how it must have felt to be one of Wellington's infantry at Waterloo.

From the Arc de Triomphe came the notes of a bugle. A hush descended on the crowds as we remembered the fallen of Verdun and Normandy, of Vietnam and Algeria. After a long two minutes the world came back to life and

I dragged the suitcase the final hundred yards over the cobbles to my hotel. I was still holding the paper flag I'd been given by a cadet to wave at the cavalry. I was about to throw it in a convenient trash bin but instead stuffed it into my luggage, a sentimental souvenir that would surely find its way to the kitchen bin when I got home.

Now as I finished unpacking, here it was in my hand. It certainly belonged in the *Before Friday* category, yet *After Friday* it had become the worldwide symbol of defiance in the face of terror. It deserved better than the recycling bin, so I stood it in the shell case that decorates my desk, alongside the Stars and Stripes that had been a gift at my US citizenship ceremony. There they stand as I write, a powerful symbol of unity, one the politicians on TV would eagerly seize upon to illustrate their brave words of patriotism and even braver threats of bloody retribution. But as an explanation for the tragedy of Paris and the conflict that grows around us, this fails a less worldly curiosity.

So I thought back to the night of the attack, retracing my footsteps—all 6.56 miles of them, according to my iPhone. Before the killing started, in the still coolness of a perfect Paris autumn evening, I made a small personal pilgrimage to the underpass at the Pont d'Alma. There was the approach road, down which eighteen years ago the world's favorite, most beautiful, and vivacious princess had sped, a long and hopefully happier life stretching ahead of her. Then I slowly made my way to the opposite parapet, its granite sanctified by the scribble of a thousand poignant felt-tip tributes. I stared down at the exit ramp, up which Diana had been carried, her dwindling life now to be measured in minutes. Across the Seine the illuminated Eiffel Tower soared into the dark sky, the searchlight at the top sweeping a long cold beam over the city, shining briefly on streets where unseen gunmen were readying their Kalashnikovs.

Oblivious, my mind was still filled with memories of visits to Paris with Diana, of her laughter as the *paparazzi* motorbikes swooped around our car like bandits round a Wild West stagecoach. I like to think she was still laughing as the Mercedes smashed into the thirteenth pillar of the underpass. With that picture occupying my mind, I wandered toward the nearest bus stop. I had my usual plan for a night alone in a friendly foreign city: ride a bus to anywhere, get off where the restaurants and cafes looked most inviting, then take a long after-dinner stroll back to the hotel.

So I got onto the first bus that came along, destination anywhere. It took me to the delights of St. Germain and oysters at Brasserie Lipp. But had I not been lost in memories and had walked a little faster, the first bus to arrive would have taken me toward the Gare de Lyon and restaurants where dozens of diners were about to be machine gunned at their tables.

By such margins do we live or die. As I lay awake that night, listening to the sirens and helicopters and hoping the mayhem wasn't about to come in my direction, it was easy to take refuge in prayer. Some scripture played on a loop in my head, connecting Verdun and Vietnam with the Alma tunnel and the carnage at the Bataclan and the Boulevard Voltaire.

Thou fool: this night thy soul shall be required of thee. (Luke 12:20)

Not required on the night of Friday 13, of this fool anyway.

But tonight? Lord, forgive our foolish ways.

December 18, 2015

51

What Death
Is Trying to Tell Us

Patrick T. Reardon

It may seem odd today, but, at one point, a half century ago, the top-selling popular song in America was made up of lyrics from the Bible—specifically, from the third chapter of the Book of Ecclesiastes.

The song, written in the late 1950s by the great folk singer Pete Seeger, was "Turn, Turn, Turn." It wasn't his version that reached number one on the Billboard Hot 100 chart on December 4, 1965. It was the rock version by the Byrds, and it began:

> To everything (turn, turn, turn)
> there is a season (turn, turn, turn),
> and a time to every purpose under
>   heaven,
> a time to be born, a time to die,
> a time to plant, a time to reap.

You might think that all the teenagers like me who were grooving to the song back then would have taken in the import of those words, particularly "a time to be born, a time to die." But we were young and felt immortal.

I think back on that song today, a year and a half after my brother David, suffering great pain and fearing to lose control of his life, killed himself during a thick shower of rain-snow outside his back door at 3 a.m. on a Friday.

David was a year younger than me, and the two of us were the oldest of fourteen children. He had had many difficulties throughout his life, and, for me and my siblings, his suicide wasn't a complete surprise.

It was a shock, nonetheless. He was here, one of us—he and I had talked just a few hours before his death—and then he was gone. There was a finality that slapped us in the face. This brother we loved was gone.

Then, just a couple months ago, my sister Eileen's husband, Bob, was killed in a boating accident. Again, the fabric of our family was ripped. Again, the realization hit us—we would never see Bob again.

Not only that, but, in both cases, there was no escaping the reminder that each one of us, like David and Bob, would one day die.

There is a Latin term for that sort of reminder, *memento mori* (remember, you must die). Back in 1958, Muriel Spark, who blended spiritual depth with a comic sensibility, published a wonderful novel with those Latin words as a title. It was about a bunch of elderly English people, mostly upper-class Londoners, who begin receiving identical telephone calls.

When they answer, the caller says, "Remember, you must die." Some are indignant. Some, amused. Some, disoriented. All are mystified.

However, Jean Taylor, a former companion-maid of one of the ladies and a former lover of one of the men, doesn't get a call. At eighty-two, she is in a government nursing home, progressively losing the use of her body to arthritis.

Jean is very aware of her declining health and approaching death. She seems to find consolation meditating on these subjects, and maybe that's why the caller never bothers with her. One chapter begins: "Miss Jean Taylor sat in the chair beside her bed. She never knew, when she sat in her chair, if it was the last time she would be able to sit out of bed."

You don't have to be eighty-two to realize that, at any moment, your life could come to an end. Dwelling on that fact may seem desolate, but, in fact, it can be life affirming.

As Americans, we live in a society that continually seeks to deny death. Look at the commercials on TV and the ads in newspapers and magazines and online, and you'd think that staying vibrantly, youthfully alive forever is only a matter of eating a certain diet and ingesting the right pills and having the perfect toys. It's all a sham, though.

To pretend that death is not somewhere on the horizon is to dwell in a fantasy existence.

However, if you remember that there is "a time to be born, a time to die," you are constantly aware that life is there to be lived.

If you know death is waiting in the wings, you know that each moment we have, each breath we take in, is precious. Each sunrise is one of only a finite number that we will have the opportunity to see. Each gentle rain. Each beautiful snowfall.

Each person we meet is a treasure. Each is dying, just as we are.

What the writer of Ecclesiastes tells us—what God is telling us—is that our job on earth is to show up. To be present. To be alive to the fullness of life, which includes being alive to the fact of death.

Here's how the poet Gwendolyn Brooks explained the job of being a human being:

> This is the urgency: Live!
> and have your blooming in the noise of
> the whirlwind.

God gives us the whirlwind in which to live. We aren't given safe, secure cocoons where we can escape the rough-and-tough of existence. We are given the storm, and we're told to blossom amid all the rain and thunder.

That reality is at the heart of last year's exhortation from Pope Francis, *The Joy of Love*. He's writing about marriage, but what he says is applicable to life in general: "Marital joy can be experienced even amid sorrow; it involves accepting that marriage is an inevitable mixture of enjoyment and struggles, tensions and repose, pain and relief, satisfaction and longings, annoyances and pleasures."

Life is that same sort of mixture of joy and sorrow, but you can't taste the joy if you're hiding from the sorrow.

Death will come, yes. But, for now, in joy and sorrow, we're called to look at the wonder of the world that God as made for us, and at all these souls sharing that world with us.

JULY 14, 2017

52

Make Sure There Are a Lot of Flowers at the Viewing

B. G. Kelley

My father knew he was dying.

From his hospital bed he looked me square in the eyes, and this now shell of a man who had once been a strapping football player—muscular and sinewy, fast as a cheetah—with a chiseled Irish mug and thick crop of black hair that made him Kennedyesque handsome, said to me, "Billy, make sure there are a lot of flowers at the viewing."

Why wouldn't he say that? For fifty years my pop was the parish florist for Corpus Christi Church and school in Philly. He believed—and imbued in me—that flowers, like sunsets, rainbows, and oceans deep, were gifts from God, and was certain, without a scintilla of doubt, that flowers played a spiritual role in death, indeed, that they represented the promise of a new and purer life by softening the harsh reality of death.

"Flowers," he once told me, "bloom beyond the tears, fears, and no next years—beyond life. Flowers are forever."

He had witnessed a thousand times the power of flowers when death brings on emotional stress. He saw how flowers brought spiritual warmth to what is, essentially, a temporal-cold occasion. Countless times in his years in the flower business he was told by the family and friends of a loved one who had passed on: "Thank you for the flowers. They meant so much to us. They were a source of strength, peace, and most of all, faith. They represented a destiny."

My pop understood the needs of his friends better than they did.

He believed—as I still do today—that flowers are important and essential spiritual guests at funerals despite the fact that an overwhelming number of death notices today call for "in lieu of," which means in place of flowers consider giving the money to a charity or an educational fund for the deceased's children. But really, in times when comfort is needed, flowers can be trusted more to provide that comfort—golden rods never fail to blaze on hills, daffodils never come up pale, roses infinitely resonate love, and chrysanthemums promise new—eternal—life.

I know all this—inherently.

You see, I worked with my pop side by side for twenty-five years in his little flower shop in a neighborhood of Philadelphia called Paradise. The accretion of memories from working with him is so sweet that I am blessed with a usable past. In difficult times, when I needed a source of strength to fill whatever holes within me need filling, I could call on those attributes of flowers: continuity, renewal, inspiration, uplift, peace, comfort, love, and yes, spirituality. Even a recent study done by Rutgers University revealed that flowers were not a luxury in angst-ridden and uncertain times, but an essential, comforting, and blissful support for dealing with our emotions.

But I didn't need science to tell me that. Flowers have always spoken to me in the verities of the heart and soul: honor, truth, love. "Strike the rock, and the water will come out of it, so that the people may drink" (Exod 17:6). It's the same with flowers. Flowers slake both secular and spiritual thirst.

So, yes, at the time of death flowers are as intimate as a whisper and immediate as a blush. They bring spiritual warmth; they bring a symbolic spiritual presence and meaning; they bring a sense of transformation, not termination.

And so it was only natural—and a law of familial legacy—that flowers frame my father's entrance into a new and purer life.

In the funeral parlor on the day that he was to be buried, I made sure his dying request would be granted. There was a bounty of flowers: a huge spray of bulbous white chrysanthemums spread the length of the casket; baskets of white gladioli shooting out of their baskets like spires stood at the head and foot of the casket; a rosary made of roses lay inside the casket; a standing bleeding heart of red carnations and twenty-five to thirty other baskets and sprays, one after another, circled the funeral parlor like a necklace.

I arranged them.

They were the other side of silence.

In the funeral parlor, after everyone had gone, I looked at my pop lying in the casket and put my hand on his as I scanned all the flowers surrounding him. The flowers reminded me of that triumphant connection: a newer, purer life emerges from of hush of death.

MAY 20, 2016

✧ SIGHTING ✧

A View from the Cross

"Father, forgive them for they do not know what they are doing."

—LUKE 23:34

53

What I Am Praying
When I Say the Lord's Prayer

Michael Leach

> *He was praying in a certain place, and after he had finished, one of his disciples said to him, "Lord teach us to pray, as John taught his disciples." He said to them, "When you pray, say:*
> *Father, hallowed be thy name. . . .*
> —LUKE 11:1–2

Pope Francis made news recently when he implied that some of the language in the Lord's Prayer needs polishing. The line "lead us not into temptation," for instance, "is not a good translation," he observed in a radio interview (*NCR*, December 11, 2017) about a new French translation of the prayer. "I'm the one who falls," the pope observed. "But it's not [God] who pushes me into temptation to see how I fall. No, a father does not do this. A father helps us up immediately."

The Lord's Prayer, or the Our Father, is my favorite prayer. I've been saying it in the words I was taught for more decades than are on a rosary. I get what the pope is talking about. But the familiar words of this prayer have become a starting point for longer meditation. Here is what I have come to see and hope to realize when I pray the Lord's Prayer:

Our Father. God is my source, my father in heaven, my mother on earth, and wherever I go, God goes too. "I live and move and have my very being in God" (Acts 17:28). God is love (1 John 4:16), and so I am literally *in love.* And God is not only *my* dwelling place (Ps 27:4) but everyone else's, too, which means our natural state is to live in peace and harmony with one another. I pray to see my neighbor today with the eye of our shared soul (Mark 12:30–31).

Who art in heaven. The kingdom of heaven is here and now, closer than breathing, nearer than hands and feet (Luke 17:20–21). I pray to realize that the purpose of prayer is not to get something or make something go away but simply to "dwell in the shadow of the Most High" (Ps 91:1), to be still and know that *I AM* is God (Ps 46: 10; Exod 3:14; John 8:58) and that we are all images and likenesses of the one *I AM* (Gen 1:27; Luke 22:19). I pray that the scales that blind me to the love that is in me and surrounds me and unites me with everyone else get swept aside like the tables at the entrance of the Temple (Matt 21:12). God, bring me into your temple and let me see (John 1:39) where you are.

Hallowed be thy name. God's signature is on everything he made. Everything in creation is a sign that points to its spiritual source: the creator of all beauty, harmony, power, and grace. I walk on holy ground (Exod 3:5). I pray to honor God's creation.

Thy kingdom come. It's come. It's in our midst (Luke 17:20–21). I can see it if I have eyes to see, I can hear its silent music if I listen to its still, small voice (Matt 13:16.) The kingdom of Love is not of this world (John 18:36). I can only see what the poet Gerard Manley Hopkins called "the dearest freshness deep down things" when I understand that the kingdom of God is not material but spiritual. To behold the reign of God requires an alchemy of the heart.

Thy will be done. This is my favorite line. My soul sometimes whispers or cries it. I need to know that God's will for me is better than anything I can imagine. Love doesn't want to hurt me. God's will is to bless me (Rom 12:2). The very first sentence of the *Catechism of the Catholic Church* teaches: "God, infinitely perfect and blessed in himself, in a plan of sheer goodness freely created us to make us share in his own blessed life." Thank you, God (1 Tim 4:4), I can relax now (Ps 23:2).

On earth as it is in heaven. Heaven is not a place far away but a quality of awareness. What happens in my consciousness manifests in my life, as words, behaviors, conditions, a mode of being in the world. The ideas I cultivate make heaven or hell. What I think of my neighbor I will do unto them, and what I do unto them I do, literally, unto myself (1 Cor 12:26). God, purify my awareness (Matt 5:8).

Give us this day our daily bread. "Jesus took bread, and when he had given thanks, he broke it and gave it to his disciples, saying, 'Take and eat; this is my body'" (Matt 26:26). I am in God because I am in Jesus, and Jesus is in me (John 14:20). I pray to feast on Jesus's life and teachings and drink of his love so that I may walk and talk and be like him. This is life eternal, to come to know God and Jesus Christ whom love has sent (John 17:3).

And forgive us our trespasses as we forgive those who trespass against us. We cannot let go of the guilt we feel born with until we see our neighbors, even our enemies, as our very self (Matt 22:39) and in forgiving them we forgive ourselves. When Jesus saved the adulteress about to be stoned, he didn't say, "Sin no more, and I will not condemn you." He said, "I do not condemn you. Now go and sin no more." Guilt makes sin, and sin makes guilt, and guilt makes more sin to escape more guilt. Forgiveness makes love and inspires us to forgive others. Love begins, and grows, with forgiveness, unearned and freely given. Forgiveness is perfect love, and perfect love drives out guilt and fear (1 John 4:18–20).

And lead us not into temptation. "When tempted, no one should say, 'God is tempting me.' For God cannot be tempted by evil, nor does he tempt anyone" (James 1:13). When we ask God for our daily bread, he does not give us a bag of stones (Matt 7:9). When temptation taunts, God lifts us up on angels' wings (Ps 91:11, 12).

But deliver us from evil. I cannot save myself; I cannot save anyone. Only Love can save us (2 Tim 4:18). I surrender my will to God's (Mark 8:35). I ask God to set me free from the destructive idea of a false self I make up in order to survive but in fact destroys me, so I may instead dwell in the shelter of the Self that sets me free (Ps 91; John 8:32). God's will is to deliver me safely into his kingdom (2 Tim 4:18).

For thine is the kingdom and the power and the glory, forever and ever (Matt 6:13). This is the last line of the Lord's Prayer in the Anglican *Book of Common Prayer*. Mikey likes it.

JANUARY 12, 2018

54

All in All, We're in Pretty Good Shape

Tom McGrath

In the months before Dad died, he gave his family an in-tensive course in *Soul Seeing*. I would visit Dad after work as often as I could in his final months. Because Dad was prepared to face his mortality head on, our visits became opportunities to plumb the depths of my own faith. One evening Dad and I were watching a ballgame neither of us was interested in so we turned it off. We sat in quiet for some time until Dad turned to me and asked, "So what do you think happens after we die? Do you believe there's a heaven?"

I knew this was not an idle question, and I took my time before responding. I had to dig deep for the truth. I didn't want to lie to my father.

"There was a stretch of time when I didn't believe there was anything after this life," I said. "But the more I come to see the pattern of dying and rising in nature, as well as in my own life, the more certain I am that this pattern will continue. I have come to trust Jesus's promise of eternal life in my gut and not just hope for it in my fantasies."

Dad took that in. After a minute of silence he slowly nodded his head. "I believe that, too," he said, and we talked about the evidence for that shared faith as experienced in our lives. That stands in my memory as the most honest and trusting conversation I ever had with my father. It opened the way to an extraordinary time of grace between us in his final days.

The Irish believe in "thin times and places," that is, places and occasions where the barrier between our physical world and the world of Spirit is so thin as to be easily breached. Dad's final month was a thin place. He began to see visitors—St. Augustine arrived frequently, as did long-deceased neighbors from the block Dad grew up on. One night Dad told me he'd had a visit from a priest from his seminary days. "He was our moral theology professor," said Dad. I asked, "So do you think he was here for your final?" Dad got the joke and we laughed until tears streamed down our faces.

One evening my daughter Patti and I arrived at my parents' home and my mother told us that it had been a particularly hard day for Dad. His pain medication was no longer effective, and the hospice nurse—an angel of mercy—was on her way with a medication that would provide more relief.

As we went into Dad's room I could see he was agitated and in pain. He greeted us with a forced smile, and it was clear he couldn't get comfortable. A short time later the hospice nurse arrived and administered the new medication. Within minutes Dad was visibly relieved. He sank back into his pillows and settled into a restful sleep. Within ten minutes he awoke, refreshed. He looked at Patti and me with a serene smile.

Dad winked at us and said, "All in all, we're in pretty good shape."

I was flabbergasted. Clearly Dad understood his situation: he was suffering a long and difficult diminishment. He had endured much suffering and many indignities, and he knew there would be more as death drew near.

And yet, here he was smiling and saying, "All in all, we're in pretty good shape." Was this just the medicine talking?

Surely the medication was a blessing and a major help to him, but the truth is that I had heard those words from him so many times before down through the decades. Through a life of prayer, Dad had been given new eyes to see that "neither death nor life, neither angels nor demons, neither the present nor the future, nor any powers, neither height nor depth, nor anything else in all creation will be able to separate us from the love of God that is in Christ our Lord" (Rom 8:38–39).

I looked over at my daughter, and I was deeply grateful she and I were present to witness this proclamation of the Gospel according to her Grandfather that Advent evening. That was Dad's message to us as we prepared for the great transition he was about to experience.

Years later, my family still recalls those words when we're tempted to believe the glass is totally empty. Someone will break the spell of the negative by smiling and saying, "Remember, all in all, we're in pretty good shape." And the truth is, we are. Nothing can separate us from the love of God. Or from one another.

AUGUST 2, 2013

55

An Eighty-Six-Year-Old Priest's Ten Resolutions for the New Year

William J. O'Malley

When we were in durance vile in seminary, unlike the prisoners in iconic stories like "The Great Escape," we didn't spend our off work hours digging tunnels under the fence to the nearest autobahn or airport. When the Thomistic proofs proved too overwhelming, Larry Madden and I wrote an annual musical. One year it was "Teahouse of the August Moon"—in which I deftly wrote the Geisha Girl offstage. Another was Heywood Hale Broun's "The 51st Dragon," which took place at a knight school not unlike our own, in which callow youth trained to face dragons name Luther, Calvin, and Barnaby. The core of the story was when one hapless knightling happens to run into a juvenile dragon and—after near terminal mutual heart attacks—they get to know one another and manage to overlook their manifold and manifest differences.

But then came what was to be our chef d'oeuvre. Let's hear it for arrogance!—a musical version of "The Odyssey." I wrote a lyric for Odysseus just as he's trying finally to escape his gilded imprisonment by Calypso. It proved to be prescient. I'm now at an age to understand I was right all those years ago:

> Shall I run and hide my fistful of stars
> Or try to harvest them all?
> Shall I sit inside secure by a hearth
> When the sky's on fire with their call?
> Just to sit and be makes a no one of me
> When the gods make the winds blow
>> fair.
> And it matters not if I find the spot.
> In the going, I'm already there.

That's where my soul's at right now.

After sixty years of taunting young minds in high schools and colleges to welcome their odysseys with imagination, fine hearts, and quick wits, I'm forcibly retired without the "aged wife" Tennyson gave my forebear. Now I age along with other beached seafarers wrapped in their own myths of what more or less were our lives. Tennyson's Ulysses exhorted his old mates:

> We are not now that strength which in
>> old days

> Moved earth and heaven, that which
>   we are, we are;
> One equal temper of heroic hearts,
> Made weak by time and fate, but strong
>   in will
> To strive, to seek, to find, and not to
>   yield.

Dylan Thomas exhorted us along with his father, "Do Not Go Gentle into That Good Night," and a great many readers and I vibrate to Willy Loman: "You can't eat the orange, and throw the peel away—a man is not a piece of fruit." And again Tennyson:

> How dull it is to pause, to make an end,
> To rust unburnish'd, not to shine in use!
> As tho' to breathe were life!

What can life legitimately keep asking of us—and we of ourselves and of life—when there's no real demand that we obey the morning alarm clock, when kids (and even grandkids) are old enough to resist intrusion, however well intentioned, when the carcass itself sends weary messages? I've learned a thing or two because I've seen a thing or two so here, for you as well as for me, are my prayers and resolutions for the New Year:

1. Help me not merely to survive but to thrive with dignity, verve, and joy.

2. Make me contagious with all the aliveness I have left in me.

3. Encourage me to be more readily forgiving, not just of others but of myself.

4. Firm up my patience with imperfection now that it's more difficult to avoid.

5. Make me both prudent and patient in yielding lest I become an amiable pushover.

6. Remind me that my caregivers have bad days, too.

7. Allow me a reasoned opinion without becoming opinion bound.

8. Sensitize me to the signals that say it's okay to ask, "How's it goin'?"

9. Keep me aware that, if I forget all this, I waste a lot of learning.

10. Remind me you had a reason to create things that eventually wear out.

Just to sit and be makes a no one of me
When the gods make the winds blow fair.
And it matters not if I find the spot.
In the going, I'm already there.

December 29, 2017

56

Everything I'd Ever Need to Know about Life I Learned from Gramma Lou

Michael Leach

"Even though you get the words right doesn't mean you get your life right." That's Leach's Law Number 27 of Religious Book Publishing. I mentioned it to my friend and author Jack Shea once and he said, "*Especially* if you get the words right!"

We read books by Catholic authors that inspire us and think, "If only we could call them up on the phone like Holden Caulfield and be their friends and maybe even hang out with them, how happy we would be!" Maybe so. But we would be in for a surprise. They can be as melancholy as the rest of us.

Henri Nouwen, for instance, was and is one of the greatest spiritual authors of all time, but he was, in his words, "a wounded healer." He was often as tortured as anyone, and his gift was in feeling our pain and applying the ointment of Jesus's teachings to our experiences. He got the words right better than anyone but was working on getting his life right all the time. Perhaps that's what it takes for us to get the words right.

The only person I ever knew who got her life right was my Gramma Lou. She was a beneficial presence who never wrote a book or gave a sermon. She smiled a lot and said little. Her favorite words to me were "Let nothing disturb you," and, "Michael, you can do all things through Christ who strengthens you." She always got the words right because she listened to you with her soul and never thought about what she was going to say next. Let me give you an example I will never forget.

My parents had divorced when I was five, right after WWII, and Gramma Lou was the harbor I could always go to, to know that I was safe. Every weekday when I got off for lunch at St. Andrew's school I'd walk through the playground to her house, and she'd make me a peanut butter and jelly sandwich and a cold glass of Bosco chocolate milk. After lunch we'd lay next to each other on the old blue sofa that smelled like my dad, and Gramma would read me a comic book. Her favorite and mine was *Blackhawk*. Blackhawk was an ace fighter pilot from World War II who gathered a motley crew around him to fight injustice. Did I tell you that my dad was a WWII pilot with more missions than *Catch 22*'s Yosarian? That he earned two purple hearts and gave them to me along with his leather fly jacket that had thirty-two little bombs painted in white on the front? He also killed Hitler with a penknife but we won't go there because nobody believed me then and you may not believe me now, but believe me, it's true. He told me.

One day lying next to Gramma Lou, I pushed the comic book down with a finger and said, "Momma Lou, I don't want to go back to school. I want to stay with you."

"We'll see," she said. "Oh, look, Chop Chop's coming through the window!"

Chop Chop was Blackhawk's sidekick. He used to be a cook and carried a butcher's cleaver. I pushed the comic down, turned on my side, and looked at Gramma Lou. "Momma Lou," I said, "you love me, don't you?" It was more a statement than a question.

She looked at me with her sweet brown eyes the color of Cracker Jacks. "Of course I love you."

"Even when I'm bad, right?"

"Yes," she smiled.

"You'll always love me, won't you, Momma Lou?"

She took me in her arms and said, "Michael, you could take Chop Chop's cleaver and chop off my arms and chop off my legs and chop off my head and throw them all in a garbage can and my head would still look at you and tell you again, *I love you!*"

That was the day I knew, without knowing, everything I'd ever need to know about God.

The corollary to Leach's Law 27, then, is that when someone has her life right, she will always get the words right, especially if they are those three little words that mean nothing unless the right person says them.

✧ SIGHTING ✧

Alyosha Kisses the Earth

Alyosha stood, gazed, and suddenly threw himself on the earth. He did not know why he embraced it. He could not have told why he longed so irresistibly to kiss it, to kiss it all. But he kissed it weeping, sobbing, and watering it with his tears and vowed passionately to love it, to love it forever and ever. "Water the earth with the tears of your joy and love those tears," echoed in his soul. In his rapture he was weeping even over those stars, shining at him from the abyss of space, and he was not ashamed of that ecstasy. There seemed to be threads from all those innumerable worlds of God, linking his soul to them, and it was trembling all over "in contact with other worlds." He longed to forgive everyone for everything, and to beg forgiveness—oh not for himself but for all men, for all echoed again in his soul. But with every instant he felt clearly and tangibly that something firm and unshakable as that vault of heaven had entered his soul. It was as though some idea had seized the sovereignty of his mind—and it was for all his life and forever and ever. He had fallen on the earth a weak boy, but he rose up a resolute champion, and he knew and felt it suddenly at the very moment of his ecstasy. And never, never, all his life long, could Alyosha forget that minute.

"Someone visited my soul in that hour," he used to say afterwards, with implicit faith in his words.

Within three days he left the monastery in accordance with the words of his elder, who had bidden him: "Sojourn in the world."

—FYODOR DOSTOYEVSKY,
THE BROTHERS KARAMAZOV,
IN *THE GOSPEL IN DOSTOYEVSKY,*
COMPILED BY BRUDERHOF

About the Writers

Jade Angelica is a Unitarian Universalist Community minister and founder and director of Healing Moments for Alzheimer's. She is the author of *Where Two Worlds Touch: A Spiritual Journey through Alzheimer's Disease* and playwright for *The Forgiving and the Forgetting: Hope and Healing for Alzheimer's*.

Claire Bangasser describes herself as a cancer survivor and a Catholic feminist who finds comfort on the margins. She has not blogged in a while now and finds her favorite praying place is in the subway. Watching people is where she finds God.

James Behrens is a Trappist monk at the Monastery of Our Lady of the Holy Spirit in Conyers, Georgia. He writes widely and well on spirituality. He is the author of *Grace Revisited: Epiphanies from a Trappist Monk*.

Sidney Callahan was one of *NCR*'s first and most popular columnists and is the author of the seminal book *Illusions of Eve*. She is an author, lecturer, college professor, and licensed psychologist. Her most recent book is *Called to Happiness*.

Alice Camille is a writer, religious educator, and retreat leader. She is the author of twenty books, including *Listening to God's Word* and other titles available at www.alice-camille.com. Alice takes God seriously and religion with a sense of humor.

Kathy Coffey is the author of popular spiritual books such as *Hidden Women of the Gospels* and *When the Saints Came Marching In*. She has four children and six grandchildren. She gives retreats and workshops nationally. Her website is kathyjcoffey.com.

Francine Dempsey is a Sister of St. Joseph of Carondelet in Albany, New York. She is a retired English teacher (College of St. Rose, Albany), member of the CSJ Justice Committee, and has been a justice advocate for many years.

Mary DeTurris Poust is the director of communications for the Diocese of Albany, the author of six books on Catholic spirituality, and a popular speaker. Visit her blog at www.NotStrictlySpiritual.com.

Brian Doyle, poet, essayist, and novelist, died too young in 2017 at age sixty from what he called "a big honkin' brain tumor." His peers said he was the best Catholic writer of his generation and one of the best essayists of any generation. His books include the novel *Mink River* and *A Sense of Wonder: Selected Essays from Portland Magazine,* which he shepherded into "the best university magazine in America" according to *Newsweek.*

Pierre Eau Claire is the pseudonym of an American poet.

Barbara Danko Garland works at Good Shepherd Montessori School in South Bend, Indiana. This is her thirteenth year as a guide in lower elementary, which includes six-to-nine-year-old children. She is married to her best friend, Brian, who is director of liturgy and music at St. Therese, Little Flower Catholic Church.

Jeannine Gramick, a Loretto sister, is a leading advocate for lesbian, gay, bisexual, and transgender (LGBT) rights and a co-founder of New Ways Ministry, a Catholic educational organization working for the reconciliation of LGBT people and the institutional church. Her books include *The Catholic Church and Voices of Hope: A Collection of Positive Catholic Writings on Gay and Lesbian Issues.* In 1995, she received the Isaac Hecker Award for Social Justice from the Paulist Community.

Patrick Jephson served eight years as equerry and the first and only private secretary (chief of Staff) to HRH the Princess of Wales. Appointed Lieutenant of the Royal Victorian Order for personal service to the sovereign, Patrick became an American citizen in 2014. He is now a consultant, journalist, broadcaster, and *New York Times* and London *Sunday Times* bestselling author.

John, a member of Al-Anon is the pseudonym of an American theologian.

B. G. Kelley is a writer and teacher who has written for the *New York Times* and *Sports Illustrated* and has authored a book of poems, *The World I Feel*. He teaches writing in a faith-based school and still arranges flowers for friends and especially for his wife of forty-six years. He is a frequent contributor to the *Philadelphia Inquirer*'s editorial page.

Gerald Kicanas, bishop of Tucson, Arizona, from 2002 to 2017, has served refugees throughout the world and was chairman of Catholic Relief Services, an agency for responding to international humanitarian need. Earlier he served as rector, principal, and dean of formation at Quigley Preparatory Seminary South and as rector of Mundelein Seminary at the University of St. Mary of the Lake.

Heather King is a former lawyer, Catholic convert, and recovering alcoholic with several critically acclaimed memoirs, among them *Parched, Redeemed, Shirt of Flame*, and *Poor Baby*. She writes a monthly column for *Magnificat* magazine and a weekly column on arts, culture, faith, and life for *Angelus,* the newspaper of the Archdiocese of Los Angeles. Her blog, Heather King: Mystery, Smarts, Laughs, is online at heather-king.com.

Mary Lou Kownacki is a Benedictine nun and writer in residence at Inner-City Neighborhood Art House. She is director of Benetvision Publishing in Erie, Pennsylvania; director of Benetvision; and director of "Monasteries of the Heart," an online monastic community (www.monasteriesoftheheart.org); and author of *A Monk in the Inner City.*

Michael Leach, publisher emeritus of Orbis Books, has edited and published more than three thousand books. In 2007, the Catholic Book Publishers Association honored him with a Lifetime Achievement Award. Dubbed "the dean of Catholic book publishing" by *US Catholic* magazine, he has also authored or edited several books of his own, including the bestseller *I Like Being Catholic* and *Why Stay Catholic?*, which won a first place award as "the best popular presentation of the faith" by the Catholic Press Association in 2012. He lives with Vickie, his wife of almost fifty years, in Riverside, Connecticut. They have two sons and two grand-twins.

Evander Lomke is president and executive director of the American Mental Health Foundation and former vice president and senior editor of Continuum International, where he managed and/or acquired twelve hundred nonfiction books for general readers as well as specialists.

Fotini Lomke is a special-education advocate who through experience in caring for their daughter has learned how to get the best help for children with special needs.

James Martin is a Jesuit priest, editor at large at *America* magazine, consultor to the Vatican's Secretariat of Communication, and the author of many bestselling books, including *Jesus: A Pilgrimage* and *The Jesuit Guide to (Almost) Everything*. He is a popular speaker and a frequent commentator on national television. A member of the LAByrinth Theater Company in New York, Fr. Jim has been a special consultant on the movies *Silence* and *Doubt*.

Tom McGrath is director of Mission & Identity at Loyola Press, learned most of what he knows from other authors included in this book, and is a frequent speaker on men's spirituality.

Michael Morwood has over forty years' experience in retreat, education, parish, and adult faith development ministries. He lives in Perth, Australia, with his wife, Maria. He is the author of many books, including *Praying a New Story* and *Prayers for Progressive Christians*.

Ginny Kubitz Moyer is the author of three books, most recently *Taste and See: Experiencing the Goodness of God with Our Five Senses*. She lives in the San Francisco Bay area "where she trips over toys, teaches high school English, and does her best to approach it all with mindfulness and humor."

William J. O'Malley, SJ, author of more than forty books, still gets letters from people who remember him as the kindly priest at the end of *The Exorcist* who made Linda Blair smile. He will always be remembered and loved by the thousands of young people he taught for more than sixty years. He is now retired and living at the Jesuit home for old super heroes at Fordham University.

Patrick T. Reardon is "a Chicago writer, born and bred," who worked as an urban affairs reporter and feature writer at the *Chicago Tribune*. He is the author of eight books, including *Requiem for David*, a poetry collection, and *Faith Stripped to Its Essence*, a literary-religious analysis of Shusaku Endo's novel *Silence*.

Mark Redmond is the executive director of Spectrum Youth & Family Services in Burlington, Vermont. He has worked with homeless and at-risk youth since 1981 in New York City, Westchester, New York, and Stamford, Connecticut. He is the author of *The Goodness Within: Reaching Out to Troubled Teens with Love and Compassion.*

Marybeth Christie Redmond is a writer-journalist whose mission is to tell compassionate stories that spark social change and give voice to people without one. She has served as director of marketing and communications for Vermont Works for Women, is a commentator for Vermont Public Radio, and is co-editor of the book *Hear Me, See Me: Incarcerated Women Write.*

Teresa Rhodes is "a sometimes author who lives in Massachusetts." Her books include *Transforming Trauma: A Spiritual Path to Wholeness* and *Mysteries of the Rosary in Ordinary Life.* Teresa has traveled the world as a consultant in mission to the poor and disadvantaged and is known for her sense of humor and compassion.

Richard Rohr is a globally recognized ecumenical teacher bearing witness to the universal awakening within Christian mysticism and the Perennial Tradition. He is a Franciscan priest of the New Mexico Province and founder of the Center for Action and Contemplation (CAC) in Albuquerque, New Mexico. His many books include *Richard Rohr: Essential Teachings on Love, The Naked Now: Learning to See as the Mystics See,* and *Everything Belongs.*

Joyce Rupp is a Servite sister, retreat and conference speaker, and author of numerous award-winning books, including *Boundless Compassion, Walk in a Relaxed Manner,* and *Joyce Rupp: Essential Writings.* Visit her website, www.joycerupp. com, for articles, prayers, poems, and other creative resources.

Heidi Russell is an associate professor at the Institute of Pastoral Studies, Loyola University, Chicago. She is the author of *The Source of All Love: Catholicity and the Trinity,* and *Quantum Shift: Theological and Pastoral Implications of Contemporary Developments in Science.*

John Shea is a theological consultant to faith-based organizations and parishes. For twenty years he directed the Doctor of Ministry program at St. Mary of the Lake University and for ten years he was the executive director of the Leadership Formation Program in Catholic Health Care at the Ministry Leadership Center. He is the author of many books, including *To Dare the Our Father.*

Maureen Sinnott, a Franciscan sister, lives in San Francisco and is a clinical psychologist. She has been giving seminars every summer in Tanzania for the past ten years. She is also on the St. Vincent de Paul Restorative Justice Advisory Board and has been offering services in the Redwood City jail for the past nine years. Currently she is serving on her provincial leadership team.

Tom Smith is co-founder, with his wife, Fran, and son Kevin, of the Karla Smith Foundation, supporting families affected by mental illness and suicide and helping them overcome mental and behavioral health challenges. He is the author of eight books, most recently *Church Chat: Snapshots of a Changing Catholic Church.*

Sue Stanton has been a journalist, nurse, and author of several books, including *Great Women of Faith: Inspiration for Action.* She is a longtime advocate for a peace organization focused on the dangers faced by Palestinian Christians. She writes from Ames, Iowa.

Fran Rossi Szpylczyn is a writer, speaker, and retreat leader with a focus on how spirituality intersects with everyday life. By day she has the privilege of welcoming God's people as the secretary at Immaculate Conception parish in Glenville, New York, and in her free moments is a beloved networker of Catholics everywhere on social media. She blogs at breadhere.wordpress.co.

Paul Wilkes founded Homes of Hope India in 2006. He is the author of over twenty books, and the host, writer, and director or producer of seven PBS documentaries. Learn how you can be part of his work in India at www.homesofhopeindia.org.

Miriam Therese Winter, a Medical Mission sister and professor of liturgy at Hartford Theological Seminary, served in Ethiopia during the famine in 1985. An award-winning musician whose songs are sung in churches across the United States, she recorded the gold record *Joy Is Like the Rain* and has written many books, among them *eucharist with a small "e."*

Joni Woelfel is the author of seven books, including *The Edge of Greatness: Empowering Meditations for Life.* She was a columnist for ten years for the *Wabasso Standard* and was a "Starting Point" contributor for *NCR.* Joni lives with her husband in Spicer, Minnesota.

Vinita Hampton Wright is managing editor at Loyola Press; a novelist; and a facilitator of workshops on creativity, writing, and Ignatian prayer. Her book *The Art of Spiritual Writing* is an essential guide. She lives in Chicago with her husband, three cats, and a dog.